Ntombi:

A Rhino's Story

Published under licence by Brown Dog Books and The Self-Publishing Partnership Ltd, 10b Greenway Farm, Bath Road, Wick, Nr. Bath BS30 5RL

www.selfpublishingpartnership.co.uk

Cover Design by pro_ebookcovers

Cover Illustration by Tracy Lee May

Copyright © 2023 Tracy Lee May

ISBN: 978-1-83952-744-9

This book is printed on FSC® certified paper.

MIX
Paper | Supporting responsible forestry
FSC® C013604

Ntombi:
A Rhino's Story

TRACY LEE MAY

DEDICATION

To all Rhino, who desperately need our protection.

MAP OF DWALA

Tracy Lee May

SAFARI LODGE

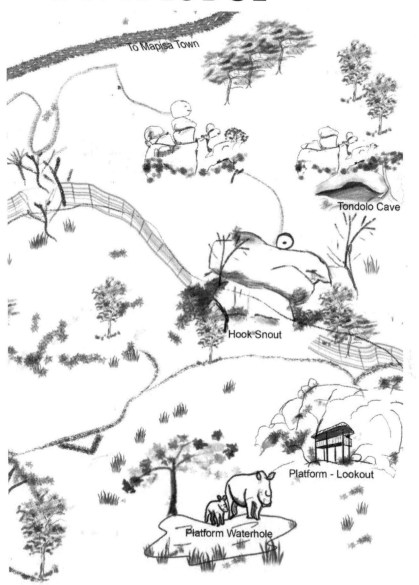

To Mapisa Town

Tondolo Cave

Hook Snout

Platform - Lookout

Platform Waterhole

CHAPTER 1

Ack, Ack, Ack!

The short cracks of gunfire silenced the African night. The Rhino's heads whipped up in unison, their trumpet ears rotating like radar.

"Phrrr," snorted Lindi, her nostrils scenting the air.

The acrid stench could only be coming from one creature, the Upright walkers that carried sticks that spit death.

Humans.

Ack, Ack, Ack!

Lindi called frantically for her companion, the bull Khulu. He'd know what to do.

"Mmmhaaa!" roared Madiba, as he charged towards the Upright humans.

Dub-dub-dub-dub-dub.

The helicopter blades sliced through the air, its searchlight landing on Khulu.

Dub-dub-dub-dub-dub. Ack, Ack, Ack!

The bull squealed and then fell silent.

Lindi's breath came in short sharp bursts as she rocked on her feet, her protruding pregnant belly heaving. Then the metal bird arched its evil bright eye in her direction, galvanizing her into action, and she bolted.

Dub-dub-dub. Ack, Ack!

Thawack. Phishh. The termite mound next to Lindi exploded, showering her in debris.

More bullets whizzed past Lindi, cracking Terminalia trees as she danced between them. In front of Lindi lay the fallen remains of the silver fence line, the fence line of the Dwala Safari Park.

As the lights of the helicopter searched for its target, Lindi leapt over the fallen fence and galloped off.

Panting, Lindi came to a halt in an open clearing, her ears constantly twitching, searching for sounds.

She swayed in exhaustion, her stomach

clenching in a contraction, and with a grunt she willed herself to move. Her baby was coming, and she needed to find safety.

The soft call of the Nightjar grew stronger as Lindi searched for her safe place. The death-spitting humans appeared to have gone, and the monolithic rocky granite giant rising out of the ground seemed to offer protection, like a sentry on guard. She knew that she had taken a huge risk following Madiba over the boundary but the smell of the sweet grasses that lay just on the other side of the broken silver fence line had been too tantalizing.

"Whoop, Whoop, Whoop," came the throaty call of Mpisi—the Hyena—the creature that follows death.

A sharp pain in her belly made Lindi groan. She touched her side with her horn.

Her baby was coming.

A dry wind blew over her damp little body as Ntombi sat shivering on the brittle grass. Her mother urged her to move, licking, nudging, and helping her get to her feet.

"Up, small one. Hurry!"

Placing a horn under her daughter's back legs, Lindi gave her newborn an encouraging nudge. Having just tentatively pushed her front feet out in front of her, Ntombi collapsed in a heap. She tried again and finally stood unsteadily on all four jelly-like legs, then took a step. She managed a weaving stagger as the rest of her tried to keep up, then with Lindi's help, she conquered her tottering legs.

"Whoop, Whoop, Whoooop," called Mpisi.

"Up! Little one, up," said Lindi to her wrinkly calf.

Crunch. Lindi spun round and scented the air before turning quickly back to her calf.

"Ntombi, we must go. Now!"

Mother and daughter weaved and swayed down the sandy track as Ntombi struggled to get the hang of her feet. Gently but firmly, Lindi all but pushed Ntombi through the thick spiky scrub, and into a safe secluded clearing, neither of them noticing the sharp white thorns that clawed at their sides. Flopping down in a puff of dust, Lindi turned to gaze at Ntombi lovingly, as the calf nuzzled her mother, looking for her first meal.

"Aah, we'll be safe here."

Gratefully, Lindi shut her eyes.

Milk dribbled down Ntombi's chin as she gazed up at the vast ebony sky stretched out above her, the distant galaxies dotted through the great dome from end to end. Shrinking back against Lindi's warm barrel-like body and breathing in her comforting scent, Ntombi's eyes widened. The sky was humongous.

In the distance, balancing boulders rose out of the ground; the large chunks of granite defying gravity as they perched precariously on top of one another.

As she nestled with her new calf, Lindi knew that her size and pointed horn were enough to protect her calf from all but one.

Humans.

CHAPTER 2

Weeks later the thudding blades of another helicopter sliced through the darkness, its headlight bright against the inky sky as it searched for the helipad of the safari lodge. Inside the cockpit, the instrument panel lights blinked, and the three passengers" faces were illuminated by the pale blue glow of their electronic devices. The smooth flight, disrupted by a sudden flash of red below, made Max, an experienced pilot, swerve sharply.

There was a loud clatter and Dexter, the thin pale boy behind Max dropped his Nintendo as he yelled into his headset. "Hey! I just got to level 15."

His stepsister, Abigail, squealed as he squashed her. "Dexter! Shove off."

"I want my Nintendo back."

Pulling on the cyclic pitch controller between his legs, Max ignored his young guests and brought the metal bird back around again, peering into the night, searching for the strange red flash. In the front, next to Max, sat the other passenger, Theodore Martin, clutching his seat with one hand and his phone in the other, whilst trying not to crinkle his expensive-looking pin-striped suit. Another jolt of the helicopter made Theodore's phone shoot out of his hand. It joined the Nintendo on the darkened floor of the helicopter.

"What's the deal, Pilot?"

"Thought I saw gunfire. Poachers are always after our Rhino."

"You'll pay for my phone if it's damaged."

"I had to check it out. Rhinos are endangered and this is close to the park boundary."

"I don't care. That phone's expensive."

At the airport, Theodore had kept them waiting for hours whilst he finished a business deal, and as a result, they'd left much later than Max liked. His suggestion that they overnight in town had met with resistance, Theodore ranting that as he was paying for this 5-star lodge, a private guide and pilot. They would fly when he said so.

Pulling the cyclic pitch controller with a sigh, Max banked and followed the dirt road, which was shining like a chalk line on a blackboard in the chopper's lights. In the distance, the tiny pinpricks of light nestled amongst the ancient granite rocks marked their destination, the safari lodge. As the chopper passed over the silver glinting boundary fence, he noticed that a section was broken, and made a mental note to tell the Safari Park Rangers when they landed.

"We're now in the Dwala Safari Park. The lodges' lights are in front of us."

With a decisive click, Dexter unclipped his seat belt to scrabble on the helicopter's floor, pushing at Abigail's legs to feel under the seats. "Where's my Nintendo? Move, Abigail."

The expertly made-up girl shoved him back.

"Getaway, Dexter. I don't know why we had to bring him. He's such a geek."

"I didn't wanna come, did I? Who wants to look at a bunch of stupid animals?"

Max glanced over at Theodore, who was staring stonily straight ahead, pointedly ignoring his squabbling children.

"Stay in your seats," said Max.

Both Dexter and Abigail ignored Max and continued to squabble. With her foot, Abigail found the Nintendo and kicked it towards Dexter, who squealed as it narrowly missed his face.

"Hey! You'll scratch the screen."

"Shut up, Dexter."

Leaning forward in her seat, Abigail thought of all the selfies she would get of her cuddling rare African animals, Dexter's Nintendo forgotten.

"Driver, what animals will we see?"

Ignoring her, Max hated it when people called him that. The girl poked him with a manicured finger.

"Hopefully, you'll see Hyena, Zebra, Baboons, Hyrax. But most people come to Dwala Safari Park for the Rhino. It is one of the few places that you will get to see these rare prehistoric animals."

"We'd better get close enough for selfies. I told my friends that I'd post them on FlikFlak."

Initially, when Theodore had suggested this trip as a way for them all to bond, she had hated the idea. Until she had seen the recent posts on FlikFlak by another girl in her year, Chloe. There was no way that Abigail was going to be left out although why they needed to bring Dexter was beyond her. Looking down at the screen on her phone, she gazed at a picture of a woman smiling at the camera, one arm around the neck of a dark bay horse. Touching the screen, Abigail thought about how she missed her and how her mother would have loved this trip. She'd always wanted to come to Africa, and now it was too late. A message pinged and she saw Chloe's latest post. Gripping her phone, Abigail glared at the screen, at a video of the other girl galloping on a horse across the African plains surrounded by Zebra. The heart symbol on the right of the screen told Abigail that the video had been seen by millions of viewers.

As she loosened her grip on the phone to hit pause, Dexter flicked Abigail's phone out of her hands, and she only just managed to catch it before it fell. This resulted in the two attempting to pinch each other, and their shouts filled the small cockpit. Theo ignored them and tried to find his phone under the seat.

This was going to be a very long safari, thought Max, stifling another sigh, wishing that he had not agreed to guide and pilot this family. He reminded himself that the money was another step closer to opening his wildlife trust.

As dawn peeked over the horizon, Kopje Lodge was illuminated with a soft hue as insects buzzed and hummed. A Cape Turtle Dove had been cooing his "work harder, work harder" call long before the sun woke, and the birdbath was already busy with small blue Waxbills and Jameson's Fire Finches, their blue and pink plumage reflecting in the water as they drank or splashed about.

A young Baboon sat in a sunlit spot on a granite rock opposite the dining room of the lodge, eyes closed, basking in the warmth as it seeped into his shaggy brown-grey fur.

Further away, the mysterious rock formations of the Dwala Safari Park transformed from darkened shadows into wonderous golden amber stone. Touches of luminous green, yellow, and orange lichen mingled with the natural charcoal greys. The sounds of the awakening bush filled the air; a distant bark from a Baboon was followed by the mournful cry of a Fish Eagle. Brightly coloured birds of all sizes and colours twittered about in the trees below the main building.

"You idiot! You unplugged my phone!" Abigail's shrill voice obliterated the chorus of birdsong. "I need to post a selfie."

"My Nintendo was flat, and I needed to get to the next level."

"I have no idea why Daddy brought you."

"I told you I didn't want to come to stupid Africa. Mother made me."

The children approached the main dining area of the lodge, and the aroma of brewing coffee and breakfast mixed with the musty scent of the awakening earth. The dining room looked different in the daylight. Gone were the glowing lanterns and welcoming fire in the firepit. Instead, all the tables were set with sparkling silverware and crisp white napkins, carefully ironed and folded. Smiling lodge staff stood against a long table laden with golden pastries and platters of colourful fruit. Still in full argument, Abigail and Dexter rudely shoved their way past the staff and ignored their cheerful greetings. They only stopped bickering when they spotted their pilot and guide, Max, who was deep in conversation with several men dressed in fatigues, one of whom had a rifle slung casually over his shoulder.

"I'm telling you, Twanda, I saw a flash of gunfire last night."

"We'll check it out. Never hurts to be too careful."

The conversation halted abruptly when Abigail and Dexter approached.

"Morning, you two. Sleep well?"

The tweens shrugged.

"Where's your father?"

"He's not MY father," said Dexter.

20

"Dunno. My phone's flat."

Taking the phone, Max plugged the phone's charger into a wall socket.

"Come. Let's eat. What would you like to do today?"

Taking a seat, his plate piled high with steaming hot pastries, Dexter stabbed the buttons with one hand as the other shovelled apple turnover into his mouth, gooey apple syrup dribbling down his chin. Out of the corner of his eye, he noticed the men-in-green walking towards the exit and looked up from his Nintendo. "Who are they? Why do they have guns?"

"They're Rangers, here to protect the Rhino."

"Can I shoot one of their guns?"

"No. They are not toys."

Pouting Dexter turned back to his Nintendo, *rat-a-tat* sounds breaking the silence at the table.

Putting her nose up at her stepbrother's eating habits, Abigail sat close to her charging phone, and took a photo of her breakfast before daintily spooning the yoghurt and fresh fruit into her mouth.

"Perhaps a game drive and a walk? Stretch your legs after the long flights," said Max.

Shrugging, Abigail grabbed her phone. Its cable stretched across the table as she shoved it under Max's nose, pushing play on the horse rider and Zebra video, followed by the same girl cuddling a Lion. "Look. Where is this? I wanna cuddle a Lion or, even better, a Rhino."

"Looks like Kenya, see there's the location tag. Can the whole world see this, Abigail?"

"Of course. If I get better shots, I'll be famous."

"But the poach—"

Max was interrupted when Theodore strode in. He pulled up a chair, sat down and clicked his fingers in the direction of the waiters, taking care not to wrinkle his Gucci safari outfit.

"You offer horse riding?"

"We do have a couple of horses here, but they are used for anti-poaching," said Max.

Ignoring Max, Theodore turned to his daughter. "How about a ride, princess?"

Abigail shook her head vigorously. It had been years since her mother's riding accident, and she'd not ridden since.

Not wanting to miss a chance at taunting his stepsister, Dexter turned to her with a grin. "You're just annoyed cos Chloe got so many likes with her galloping Zebra post."

Abigail thrust her face in his. "Shut up Dexter. Who asked you?"

"You scared, are you?"

"Daddy, make him stop."

With a smug smile, Dexter turned back to his Nintendo.

Abigail turned back to her father with a huff. "Why did you bring him? He's such a geek."

"Because he's your brother," said Theodore.

"STEP. My stepbrother."

Running a hand over his face, Theodore glared at his daughter, but when he spoke again, his voice was softer.

"Be nice, Abigail. If you're not gonna ride anymore, I'm gonna sell that pony."

"You can't—he was Mummy's. She loved him."

Not looking up from his Nintendo, Dexter taunted. "And look where that got her."

Choking back a loud sob, Abigail turned on her stepbrother, her face red. A jingle from Theo's pocket interrupted them and he frowned at

Dexter before leaving, phone in hand. Abigail gave a sniffle and stared at her clenched hands.

With an embarrassed smile at the other guests—most of whom were staring at the children, annoyed—Max took in the girl's outfit of stark white shirt and minuscule psychedelic pink hot pants. "Abigail, do you have some more suitable clothes?"

"Why?"

"Well, that's not suitable for a safari."

"Why not? This outfit is the latest in fashion from Chillers."

"Wildlife will spot you a mile away if you wear white. Also, unless you want to be bitten by Tsetse Flies, Ticks, or Mozzies, I would suggest covering up a little."

"Fine."

As Abigail flounced off in the direction of the room she'd been forced to share with Dexter, Max noticed Dexter's feet—the boy was wearing bright blue Crocs.

"Dexter, your clothes are okay, but you have to change into trainers or boots."

The boy didn't look up from his console and after several attempts to get his attention, Max gave up.

Dropping into a chair, Abigail returned, and smiled defiantly at Max. Now wearing a brown blouse, the revealing shorts remained. "Daddy said I look fine."

Behind her trailed Theodore, the phone still to his ear, his hair spiked from his habit of running his hands through it.

"Yes. Of course. Our guide said we should see them," Theodore looked up when he spotted Max and lowered his voice, "Yes. I'll text you the location. I won't let you down."

"Did you get breakfast, Theodore?" asked Max.

With a grunt, Theodore took a gulp of coffee.

"No breakfast. Never touch it."

Max pushed his chair away from the table.

"Right. Let's go. Hopefully, we'll get to see Rhino."

Thumping his mug down, Theo followed the guide, and the youngsters trailed behind.

With Dexter's nose glued to his Nintendo, he slammed into a waiter laden with a tray full of bacon and eggs. The waiter and his heavy tray wobbled as he tried to avoid the boy but to no avail. The tray narrowly missed Dexter's head and went sailing through the air, landing on the red polished floor with a crash. The rest of the guests looked up at the sound and the waiter's cry of alarm.

Meanwhile, Dexter carried on unabated, thumbs punching the Nintendo to the sounds of gunfire.

Waking with a start, Lindi struggled to her feet, certain that she'd heard the thud of that terrifying metal bird. With a sigh, Lindi remembered that it had been weeks since the night of Ntombi's birth. Turning, she stared at her sleeping little daughter, who still had tinges of pink on her wrinkled grey body, three perfect toes on each foot, and long dark eyelashes which fluttered against her cheeks in the wind. She watched as the rays of the sun chased away the scary shadows of the night, and then with a gentle nudge she woke Ntombi, who blinked against the brightness of the rising sun.

"Come on, little girl. Have some breakfast."

Lindi stepped out of their hiding spot, and Ntombi followed her mother, nuzzling at her side, hoping for more milk. With a chuckle, Lindi paused long enough to let her daughter suckle. Nuzzling into her mother's belly, Ntombi slurped noisily, finishing with a great loud rumbling burp. She gazed out from under the safety of her mother's belly, taking in the tall, towering balancing boulders and others that were smooth and domed. The world seemed friendlier in the subdued light of early dawn until she noticed a huge menacing granite boulder seemed to be glaring down at her. It rose out of the thick vegetation like a monster, with a pointed snout for a nose and an angry scowling face.

"Come along, Ntombi. Mama's turn for breakfast."

Keeping one eye on the hook-beaked gigantic rock, Ntombi trotted after her mother, trying to see over the tall yellow grass.

"What's that scary thing, Mama?"

"Rocky giants. There are many around our home."

Among the crisp, sepia-coloured grasses, Lindi spotted tasty green shoots—a great find at this time of year, when all around was dry and dusty.

Nearby, a small trickle of water emerged from the diminished riverbed and fed the grass. Lindi tucked in with relish.

Close by, Ntombi leapt and bound around the open grasslands, tripping over her large round, three-toed feet, quite forgetting that she was new to this walking thing. Then she noticed a large shape attached to her feet. Lifting one foot, she squealed as the shape copied her. Leaping and jumping she tried all she could to make it disappear. No matter what she did, the shape copied and followed her. Puffing in the dust cloud, Ntombi stamped her feet in frustration, but her shadow refused to budge. "Go away."

"Ntombi, stop that. All that dust will make you—"

"Aachoooo."

Ntombi landed on her bottom with a thud, a startled look on her face.

"—Sneeze," finished Lindi chuckling. "Oh, Ntombi. Silly little Lumber-beast."

Turning to look behind her, hoping that the sneeze had chased her shadowy shape away, Ntombi clambered back to her feet and ran to her mother, who was still eating.

"Mama, make it go away."

"It's just your shadow. See? I have one too."

"What's a Bumber-beak?"

"Lumber-beast. It's what we—"

Not waiting for her mother to finish her sentence, Ntombi bolted off again, chasing her shadow, getting farther and farther from her mother, as she twirled and leapt, delighting when the shadow did the same.

"Ntombi! Wait!"

Ntombi ignored her mother, racing away, a cloud of dust trailing behind her.

"Come back here!"

Breathlessly, Lindi chased after her daughter.

"It's not safe."

Ntombi heard a soft whining coming from a tree, and she wandered curiously over to it, forgetting all about her ranting mother. The sound stopped. But when she took a few steps back, the whining buzz restarted. Back and forth went Ntombi, puzzled by the strange whine from the Shade-giver—Ntombi had, up until then, thought that trees were silent. She moved closer to the Shade-giver, determined to find it.

The Cicada continued to taunt Ntombi, buzzing when she moved away, and stopping when she moved closer. Ntombi put her wide snout on the thin branch of the tree and started to sniff. As her huge nostrils took in great gulps of air, the camouflaged insect gave up and flew off.

"Ntombi! Listen to me!"

"Sorry, Mama."

"Maiwe, you are going to be the death of me," Lindi sighed at her headstrong daughter. "Come, Ntombi. The noisy whiney bugs are out, it means it's getting warm, and it is time for our snooze."

"Why? I'm not sleepy."

"Lumber-beasts always snooze when it's hottest."

"Why?"

"It's cooler to move during dark time."

"Why?"

"It just is."

CHAPTER 3

Easing her hefty grey body down under some stunted thorn trees, Lindi sighed and rested her wide snout on the ground. Her breath created a puff of dust as she closed her eyes. A reluctant Ntombi ambled up behind her mother—she didn't want to rest. Then she noticed the strange plant; thin, its small green leaves hanging off it, with one or two sickle pods that could just be seen.

"I wonder what that tastes like?"

She opened her mouth and tugged on the green leafy stick thing.

"Yuck, PAH!" She quickly spat it out again.

The stick thing whipped back and with a resounding thwack, whacked Lindi on her leathery butt.

"Oomph! Stop that, Ntombi!"

A slow smile stretched over Ntombi's face, and she pulled back hard on the stick again.

"I'm warning you, Ntombi."

The baby stared into her mother's face, stick still in her mouth.

"Ntombi!"

She pulled the branch back further until it gave way, breaking in two with a loud CRACK.

The sound echoed like a gunshot through the valley. Lindi leapt to her feet, her eyes wild and head swaying. Ntombi gazed at her mother in shock and shrank away from her. Noticing the cracked stick, Lindi relaxed and huffed.

"Enough, Ntombi."

Pouting, Ntombi thumped down next to her mother. "I'm bored."

She heaved a sigh looking about for a suitable plaything. An eerie ringing cry echoed through the valley of granite rocky giants, where the two Rhinos lay.

"Weeee-ah, oh oh oh".

Ntombi jumped up alarmed.

Lindi was relieved to recognise the call of her Fish Eagle friend and smiled as she saw her shadow glide over the tan colour grass in front of them.

"Sounds like the flapper, Farai. She's a Fishy-catcher."

"Fishy-catcher?"

Knowing that she would not get her nap if she didn't stop Ntombi's rapid line of questions, Lindi answered in a gush.

"A huge flapper eats fish and flaps above us. A fish is a creature that lives in our drink. NOW GO TO SLEEP!"

Lindi rested her head back down, eyes closing, ignoring her youngster. A Baboon's bark reverberated through the granite hills, bouncing between the rocks, sounding much nearer than they were.

"Waahu, Whaa Huu."

"Mama, what's that?"

"Hmm," mumbled Lindi sleepily, "Just noisy Wahu's."

"Why are they called Wahu's, Mama?"

Clambering over her mother's head, Ntombi tried to get her attention.

"Just listen," Lindi turned from side to side, trying to get her bouncy daughter off her head.

"Waahu, Waahu."

Cocking her head, Ntombi listened intently to the call. Finally, she settled down again with her mother. "Hook-snout is glaring at me, Mama."

Lindi looked at her little calf, nudging her gently with her horn. "It's nothing to fear."

Gazing out towards the vista in front of her, Lindi took in the giant that Ntombi called Hook-snout. She knew that it and the other boulders weren't menacing, but rather like a comforting old friend. The dry wind swirled around, making the rusty dried leaves of the Mopane tree flutter around the pair like Butterflies.

Suddenly, Lindi caught a whiff of a pungent scent and she leapt to her feet, startling Ntombi who was finally drifting off to sleep. Rotating her ears, each one flicked about in different directions, trying to hear what could be out there. Taking a few steps forward. She sniffed and moved protectively towards her youngster, then lifting her great head again, horns poised, she gave a snort, spinning on her hind legs.

A loud shout reached Lindi's ears.

Humans!

Shoving Ntombi out in front of her, Lindi's heart thudded in her barrel-like chest.

"Run, Ntombi!"

"This is boring!" said Dexter loudly.

Kicking at the dust and fallen leaves, he reached into his pocket for his Nintendo, wailing when the device refused to respond.

"Argh! Low battery!"

They stood in a semi-circle around Max, as he pointed to a small plant that crept along the ground, a pink trumpet-like flower, and an oval fruit with two devil-looking thorns pointing upwards.

"This is Devil's Thorn, not great for car tires, but is used as a soap. Look, I'll show you."

Max rubbed the small plant together in his hands and poured a splash of water on top. As he rubbed a clear goo oozed from the leaves and dribbled between his fingers. Wrinkling her nose, Abigail stepped away from it as Max tried to hand it to her.

"Try it, Abi. It's completely natural and dries on its own, leaving no sticky residue. Want to give it a go, Dexter?"

Shoving his Nintendo into his back pocket, Dexter opened his hand tentatively towards the gloopy substance in Max's hand. "Hey. It does work."

"It sure does. My wife uses it as a shampoo and skin softener."

It had been a few hours since breakfast and the group were on their first game drive through the park. The coolness of the morning had been replaced by scorching dry heat as the Cicadas hummed, and the tiny Mopane Flies buzzed around the faces of the sweaty tourists.

"It's hot. Why won't these Flies leave me alone?" whined Abigail.

"They're a stingless Bee, they're after your sweat to make honey. It's rather delicious if you are lucky enough to find any."

"Eeww," muttered Abigail.

Chuckling, Max moved to walk away and noticed some tracks. "Look here. Rhino tracks. A female with a calf. Looks like we disturbed their lunchtime nap."

Giving a frustrated huff, Theodore turned on Max, waggling his finger in his face. "Enough about piles of dung, dusty markings, irritating insects, and stupid green twigs. Travel Agent promised the big five and WHERE ARE THE RHINO?"

"This is not a zoo," replied Max.

Rubbing his temples, Theodore looked at the guide grumpily. "What is that annoying whine, like a million tiny jet engines? It's giving me a headache."

"Those are Cicadas, a remarkable camouflaged insect, they—Wait! Shhh—"

Max stopped abruptly as he spotted a large grey shape lumber through the thick tangle of Acacia shrubs.

"They what?" said Abigail, mid-selfie.

"Shh—Look! There! Rhino!" said Max.

"Brilliant! A Rhino selfie!" Abigail whooped as the phone's camera whirred.

Just then Theodore's phone jingled loudly from his pocket.

"Yes. Okay. Will send—Hello? Hello? Argh, no signal."

Frightened by the loud jangle and shout, the Rhino gave a snort and crashed through the scrub as they fled, leaving the guide peering into the russet-coloured bushes.

With a gasp, Abigail brandished her phone under her father's nose. "Look! I got it. I got a photo of the baby. Oh, how cute!"

Ignoring his daughter, Theodore shoved his daughter out the way and brandished his own phone as he paced back and forth. "I need to get the signal back. NOW!"

Ignoring Theo and stepping towards Abigail, Max held out his hand. "Let's look, Abi. Great shot. Well done."

"Take us back," said Theodore with a huff.

Handing the phone back to the girl with a sigh, Max looked back in the direction of where they last saw the Rhino.

"Well, that's all we're gonna see of that Rhino now that we've frightened her. Let's head back."

"Good, when I've posted this. I'm gonna work on my tan by the pool."

As he climbed into the driver's seat, Max turned to Abigail, a serious look on his face.

"Abigail, I hope that you remembered to switch your phone to flight mode as I asked you to in the safety talk earlier?"

"Yeah, yeah. Of course."

"Are you sure?"

"I said I did. Okay."

Satisfied he turned the key in the ignition and as he inched the vehicle forward, Max could make out the sounds of gunfire from Dexter's Nintendo as he killed yet another Zombie.

The dust trailed behind the dark green Land Rover, as they bounced along the rutted dirt track of a road.

The grass and bushes that grew in the middle

brushed and scraped against the underbelly of the Landy.

"If I go any faster, Theo, the kids will be flung from their seats,"

"Got to send this message. It's important."

Ignoring Theodore, Max slowed for yet another rut in the dirt road, knowing that the kids in the back were having a tough time staying in their seats. Keeping his eye out for the Zebra and Wildebeest herds that were often seen in this area, they came round another bend—and there they were.

Slowing the truck further, he heard the click of the phones from the back. A loud huff from Theodore had Max put the truck back into gear to drive off again.

"The Park has a very strict speed limit but there's the lodge now."

The vehicle had hardly come to a standstill and Theodore was out of it, brandishing his phone like a sword.

Abigail clambered down the ladder on the side of the safari vehicle and trotted after her father. "Daddy. Come sit by the pool."

"Hello. Yes. I'm here. The blasted place has terrible signal." Strutting up the granite steps toward the main building, phone now firmly attached to his ear, Theo's loud voice brought the staff running from the kitchen in a panic; the game drive wasn't supposed to be back for another hour. The table still had to be set for lunch.

"Yebo Max, is everything okay? You're back early."

The lodge manager had joined his staff to find out what all the fuss was about.

"Ja. Had a brief sighting of a Rhino but Theo wanted to come back for the Wi-Fi."

"Brunch won't be for an hour or so, but I can arrange for some snacks in the meantime."

"Thanks. Perhaps the kids can have a drink by the pool until then.

Turning back towards Abigail and Dexter, Max noticed they were already heading up the steps, one pouting and posing in front of her phone and a loud *rat-a-tat-tat* could be heard from the games console.

With a big shrug, Max turned back to the manager. "Some people, Vusa. To pay all this money but have no interest in the experience. Perhaps this afternoon's sundowners at the platform overlooking the waterhole may entertain our guests?"

"He's a stockbroker, isn't he? Show them a good time and the lodge should get good reviews."

Just after brunch, Theodore pulled Max aside. "I have work to do. Ensure that Abi and Dexter are entertained this afternoon. I do not want to be disturbed," Theo turned on his heel and stomped off towards the youngsters, calling out loudly to get their attention.

"Oi! Abi, Dexter! Daddy must work this afternoon. But Max here has said he has a great afternoon planned for you."

"Not again. All you do is work," said Abigail, her voice rising above the hum of the other guests.

Noticing the girl's quivering bottom lip and brimming eyes, Max hastily glanced around at the other guests who were chatting about their upcoming safaris, a mixture of accents filling the room.

Smiling apologetically at a blond German woman who looked up frowning at the loud voices, Max quickly avoided another scene. "We'll head to the platform, I think. You will need to change though, guys, as we'll come back after sunset and this time of year it is quite cold at night."

"It's practically boiling. I'm not putting warm clothes over this cute outfit."

The girl had changed yet again and was sporting an ensemble of a blue crop top and shocking pink camo hot pants.

"I thought I told you to cover up—and blue is not a great colour either. Attracts Tsetse Flies."

"I'm not changing again."

"Suit yourself. Don't say I didn't warn you." Turning towards the boy, Max noticed that he was still wearing the blue Crocs. "Dexter, don't you have trainers or hiking boots?"

The boy just shrugged and stared down at his phone. Walking off towards the lodge's office, Max shook his head. This was going to be a very long safari. Just think what the money from this trip will mean to the wildlife trust, he reminded himself.

CHAPTER 4

Ntombi was settling with her mother in the
shade under the overhang of a granite boulder,
providing much-needed shelter from the heat of
the day. Trees were bare of leaves at this time of
year. As Ntombi eased her bottom down, she
noticed strange markings on the grey rock next to
her. It was a dark red colour, not at all like the
colour of the luminous green or orange lichens that
grew on the rocks.

Stepping a little closer Ntombi noticed that one even looked a little like the shadow that followed her, she gave the strange shape a sniff, the granite felt a little cool on her snout but otherwise smelt the same as always.

"Mama. What dis?"

"Hmm. It's just rocky giants, you know that."

"But what's this shape?"

"Dunno. There are many with these strange markings. Now have a nap."

Growing bored with the shape when it stubbornly refused to move, Ntombi eased her backside down next to her mother and was soon dreaming of her favourite snack. A dream so vivid; she was soon making slurping sounds with her square, wide lips. The sun was high and bright in the sky and beat down on the already parched landscape.

Behind her, Lindi's lips were softly snorting as she slept, little puffs of dust floating up in front of her horn.

Leaping up in surprise when something landed on her back, Ntombi could feel sharp little claws digging into her sensitive hide.

"Chirrup, chirrup."

Shocked at this small dusky brown bird, who had the audacity to use her as his perch, she gave a squeal when he pecked at her skin.

"Excuse me!!"

"Hi, I'm Tubiso, but my friends call me Tubi."

"Not your friend—"

Before Ntombi could finish, the pesky critter had dived inside her ear. "HEY!!"

Flicking her ear angrily, Ntombi tried to shake off the persistent little pest.

Popping back out from the depths of her funnel-like ear, he hopped over to her other ear and peered inside.

"Where are all the Bite-yous?"

Ntombi shook her head again, as Tubi's chirp echoed in her ears.

"Make it go away, Mama."

"Hello, Tubi. Ntombi is too young for your tasty treats. I'm sure I have tons. Help yourself."

With a flutter and an excited chirp, Tubi abandoned Ntombi for her mother and dived into Lindi's ear, re-emerging a few minutes later with two fat juicy Ticks in his beak.

"Thanks, Lindi. Those were yummy. Have any more?"

Lindi smiled as the little bird hopped about on her head, checking her other ear and then her nostrils. "You're welcome, Tubi. Your mother about?"

"Yebo," replied Tubi.

Just then another little bird, covered in dusky brown feathers but with a flaming and yellow beak, landed on the top of Lindi's horn.

"Yebo, Izzy. How've you been?"

"Lindi, it's been a while. Look at your beautiful little one."

Lindi looked at Ntombi with pride, as her child busily huffed and flicked her ears trying to dislodge Tubi, who was hopping about on the top of her head. "Oh, she is. But she is such a little skelim. Too naughty."

More head shaking from Ntombi, followed by a little leap. "Get off!"

Ignoring Ntombi's huffing and puffing, Tubi continued his hunt for Ticks and other Bite-yous. Hop. Hop. Hop. Peck. Peck.

Eyes popping open, Ntombi leapt to her feet with a huff trying to dislodge the little bird who had crept under her tail and pecked at a spot on her bottom. "WHOA! Get away from there!"

As Ntombi sat down with a thud, her tail tucked firmly over her bottom, Tubi just managed to get out from under the massive expanse of the grey rump.

"Hey!" Squawked Tubi, his mouth full of Bite-yous. "You almost squished me."

Looking from Ntombi's sulky face, with her bottom firmly placed on the floor, to the small flapper chirping angrily above her, Lindi and Izzy both started to laugh. "Hehe. Ntombi you are a funny little thing."

Giving a shocked screech, Tubi flew up to a nearby Acacia tree.

"LITTLE! She's not little from my point of view."

"Phfft! Hahaha! Leave Tubi alone, Ntombi."

Luckily, Tubi was not one to let a little thing like a large bottom spoil his appetite and he soon forgot his indignation, diving back onto Ntombi, this time under her belly.

Trying to ignore the irritating pest, Ntombi wandered back over to her mother, disgusted.

"Tubi will be a good friend if you let him and will help get rid of the Bite-yous."

"Why? What's a Bite-yous?"

"A nasty critter that attaches to your softest flesh and sucks at you."

"Don't like anything there," grumbled Ntombi.

"Look. Izzy and I are good Shamwaris."

"Eh he, we are good friends," agreed Izzy.

With that, Lindi wandered off to lie under the shade of a cluster of small silvery-leafed trees, nattering to Izzy as the feather-flapper mimicked her son, flitting in and out of Lindi's ears.

All afternoon, Tubi persisted in his irritation of Ntombi and his pursuit of his delicious Bite-yous, so much so that Ntombi gave up trying to nap and wandered about, feeling the long swishy tan grasses tickling her tummy.

Suddenly, Tubi and Izzy flapped up into the air. "DANGER! DANGER! Tsk, Tsk, Kirrr."

Up Lindi leapt, huffing, puffing, snorting, and trying to see or smell what had startled the Oxpeckers, Izzy and Tubi.

Then Ntombi saw the strangest creature. It clattered and rumbled over the bumpy track, a cloud of dust trailing behind it. With a screech the green truck came to a sudden halt and suddenly gave birth to more strange creatures.

Ntombi took a few curious steps towards the upright-looking animals, sniffing as she went. As the first two humans crouched down, Ntombi stepped closer, struggling to get a better look at them, quizzically staring at the fascinating creatures. The last one was even stranger with a funny small device in its hand that made clicking sounds. With an angry huff, Lindi stepped in front of her daughter.

"NTOMBI! Let's go!!"

"Mama? What are these?"

"Uprights. Let's go."

Her mother gave Ntombi a shove, making her move in front of her and broke into a run heading away from the crouched humans, Izzy and Tubi flapped furiously above them and shouted their warning as they flew. Reluctantly, Ntombi moved swiftly away from the interesting Upright-standing animals, her mother close behind.

A loud chattering voice could be heard from behind them.

"Man! Look at them go. I would get to the next level if I had that speed."

A while later, when Ntombi thought that they would never stop running, they came to a clump of shade-givers, the ones with the flutter-fly leaves.

From their vantage point in the sky both Izzy and Tubi said that they could not see any more danger and Ntombi gratefully flopped down. She had missed her midday nap and was ready for it now.

"Thank you, Izzy and Tubi, for the warning," said Lindi, addressing their two feathered friends. "You see Ntombi, Tubi will be a great friend."

"But why did we run Mama?"

"They are dangerous, little one."

"But they looked like fun."

Ignoring her daughter, Lindi huffed, and the dust puffed in front of her, like a grey cloud.

"Mama?"

"Hmmm."

"What were those things?"

"Uprights. The only creature that looks and smells like that."

"They did smell funny. Where were all their legs? Don't they fall over?"

"Hehe. They don't look steady on those sticks. But be warned: they are dangerous."

"Didn't look dangerous. You just don't want me to have any fun."

Mumbling, Ntombi started to drift off to sleep.

"No time for a nap, little one. We're going to the waterhole. Now, up you get."

Slowly, the Land Rover inched down the road, Max keeping a sharp eye out for any wildlife, as well as footprints left behind in the dirt.

Behind him sat the two sulking youngsters, Dexter muttering about his games console. "I want my Nintendo. I'd better not lose my place on the leaderboard. I'm in the Top Ten."

"Well, my phone's okay. I can still take selfies," Abigail said.

Dexter kicked the back of the seat in front of him, which just happened to be the driver's seat.

The impact of each kick flicked Max's head forward until he brought the Land Rover to a stop, turned to Dexter, and told him in no uncertain terms not to do that again.

Turning back, Max noticed footprints that crossed the dirt track. Leaping over the half-door—it had been halved when the roof was removed to make it into a safari truck—he crouched down to inspect the marks in the sand.

Max said in a hushed voice, "Look here guys! Rhino tracks. See the large one and then the smaller set. White Rhino. See the indent on the back pad, Black Rhinos don't have that. This fresh print shows the three toes."

Rolling his eyes, Dexter scoffed and crossed his arms across his chest. "More tracks."

Looking up from her phone mid-selfie, Abigail leaned over the side and took a shot with the Rhino prints in the background. "He's obsessed with them. Max, you sound like that wildlife chap on the TV. You know, the really, really old one."

"Shhh. Quiet. I hear something," said Max.

"Tsk Tsk Crr."

The alarm call from the bushes to the side of them had Max spinning round.

"It's an Oxpecker. They feed off the Ticks and fleas on larger mammals like the Rhino. Come, let's see if we can get closer. Remember the safety talk from yesterday?"

Neither of them answered. Max took a deep breath and explained again that the best thing to do if a Rhino charged them was to stand still. In extreme circumstances, he told them to climb a tree.

Scoffing, Dexter pointed to Max's rifle that lay across the windshield of the truck still in its bag. "Why not just shoot it with your big gun, Max? Isn't that your job—to protect us?"

"I don't want to shoot a Rhino in self-defence, but I will protect you. If you listen to me, we'll be fine."

Pouting into her phone Abigail took a picture of the Land Rover behind her, and then held it ready to take her first selfie with an animal. A photo with a Rhino would surely double her "Likes" on social media.

Dexter, on the other hand, looked about him nervously. He was certain that he was going to be eaten by some wild beastie and would have preferred to stay at the lodge getting to the next level.

"Right then, let's go," whispered Max.

With a sigh, the children reluctantly fell in behind their guide, Max, just as they had been told in the safety talk. Hunching over, they crept through the bush as quietly as they could. Even so, their footsteps still crunched on the dry grasses and fallen leaves. Max followed the Rhino tracks as they weaved through the trees. To Abigail and Dexter, the walk seemed endless until Max cautiously led them around a dusty grey thorn bush and crouched low to the ground, pointing at two shapes not too far away.

In a hushed tone, still pointing Max said, "See there? Near those thorn trees. These are White Rhino or more accurately Wide-lipped Rhino, they are the largest of—"

Suddenly, the mother Rhino lifted her head, snorted, and lead her calf away from the humans at a gallop, the Oxpeckers flapping behind them furiously. Watching them flee, Abi looked at her phone and realised that her finger was still on the shutter button.

"I got the whole thing! Let's follow them!"

"Sorry, Abi. Don't want to stress the mother. Let's talk more at the vehicle."

Turning on his heel, he led the way back to the truck, the kids trailing behind him, kicking up the dust as they did so. Stopping along the trail, Max pointed to a steaming pile of dung, its whiffy smell wafting around them. Holding their noses and breathing noisily through their mouths, the kids peered down.

Pointing at the pile, Max said, "Look."

Abigail shrieked, "It moved!"

Max dug through the dung to reveal a large shiny black Beetle. Holding it around its middle between his thumb and middle finger, whilst the Beetle squirmed and wriggled to free itself, Max explained that it was a Dung Beetle or Scarab Beetle.

"It stinks," said Dexter, still holding his nose.

"It's in dung, you idiot," said Abigail.

"Ja. Look. See how it rolls a ball," said Max, pointing to another Beetle who had rolled a rather large ball.

"Why does it do that?" asked Dexter.

"It's what's called a nuptial ball. A single egg will be laid in it and when the larvae hatch, a year later, it will eat the dung from the ball."

They watched as the Dung Beetle rolled the ball over and over, pushing with his powerful front legs that looked a little like he'd been pushing weights, and stopping every so often to pat it smooth.

"There's another on the other side.".

"That's his wife. He made the ball for her—and to think I had to give my wife a diamond ring," said Max with a grin.

Placing the Beetle back on the pile of dung, they continued down the track.

The next minute, Abigail let out an almighty squeal. "AAAH! What's biting me?"

Max turned hurriedly back suspecting the worst—this was Africa after all—to see Abigail trying to swat a large brownish Fly that had attached itself to her calf. Quickly, he grabbed the offensive beast and flicked it onto the ground. The Fly shook itself and flew off.

"It's a Tsetse Fly. Their bite is nasty."

Searching his surroundings quickly, Max found what he was looking for. A strange insignificant-looking shrub, with tiny leaves and sharp offensive-looking thorns or spikes. Max snapped off a branch and carried it over to Abigail as he crushed a few leaves in his fingers.

"Here, rub this on the bite. It's anti-inflammatory and should help."

"Gross. What is it?"

"It's commonly called Sickle Bush, because of the sickle-shaped pods it gets. See, there are still a few pods. These spikes can be horrendous on car tires though."

Back in the truck, Abigail rubbed the green concoction on a lump about the size of a large grape that was already forming on her calf and stuck her tongue out at a grinning Dexter.

"Should've listened to Max, Princess."

"Don't me call that. You nerd."

As they drove away, Dexter spotted a stark white object in a clearing just off the road. "What's that?"

Bringing the truck to a stop, Max turned in his seat to see what Dexter was pointing at. Littered over a small area of the clearing were bones of various sizes, but the whopping skull was what Dexter had spotted.

"Rhino carcass. It was poached about a year ago. Look, you can see where the horn was hacked off with a machete. There's an area outside of the park fence where the poachers managed to massacre several Rhinos; the carcasses lie there still, their life force gone. It is heart-wrenching."

"That's awful," said Abigail.

"What do they want the horn for?" asked Dexter.

"Some people believe that it contains medicine."

"Does it?" asked Abigail.

"No. It's just like our hair and fingernails made of a substance called keratin. If we aren't careful, your grandkids will only see Rhinos in books; just like dinosaurs and the dodo."

This shocked them into silence until they reached the viewing platform, racing up the stone steps when Max told them that drinks and snacks were at the top. Screaming and shouting, pushing, and shoving at each other, they arrived at the top gasping.

When the other lodges' guests turned and looked at them with disgust, Max looked at them sternly and put a finger to his lips. "Quiet, guys. You'll frighten the wildlife."

The platform was a stone thatched building, nestled in amongst an outcrop of granite rock formations that had a marvellous view of the Dwala Safari Park. Directly below was a waterhole, that many of the park's wild inhabitants frequented. This was why Max had brought his young guests here, in the hope that they would spot something that would ignite a spark in their interest.

Turning back to the children and gesturing behind him, he said, "The Dwala Safari Park was established in 1926 and has a wide diversity of flora and fauna. Boasting over ninety mammal species, a hundred and eight species of birds and over two hundred different types of trees and flowers."

Both Dexter and Abigail had a cold Cola in their hands and were greedily tucking into the snacks that Vusa had provided for them.

Stuffing a mini pizza in his mouth, Dexter mumbled, "Birds and flowers are boring."

"Steady on, guys. There's plenty to go around," said Max.

"We don't eat pizza at home, even mini ones," said Dexter.

"That's coz I need to eat properly," said Abigail, "I don't want to look fat on my profile."

"Yeah, well. I don't care."

Covering the awkwardness and seizing the only moment when his young guests had other things in their hands other than their electronic devices, Max turned to face the unusual vista in front of them and said, "Most people expect Africa to be open grass plains with flat-topped trees and an impressive animal under each one. But it's a vast continent with scrubland, deserts, mountains, and lush jungles."

"These rock formations are weird," added Abigail, who put her drink down to pick up her phone for yet another selfie. The setting sun made the sky look like it was on fire, so vivid were the colours.

"These hills were formed millions of years ago by weathering—not volcanic activity—and may have been home to man and beast since the stone age. The San people even left behind their rock art. I can take you to a few caves with good paintings if you're interested."

More photos followed as the sun continued to dance in front of their eyes.

"When I bring my son to this park, we love to look at the shapes and make faces and creatures out of the rock formations. See that one in the distance that looks like it has a hooked beak for a nose? We call it hook-snout,"

"Just like Dexter's beak," taunted Abigail.

"Well, you're—"

"Quiet, you two. Look!"

Across the open plain, the lanky flaxen grasses parted, revealing a bouncing Rhino calf and her ever-watchful mother coming up behind.

"It's the Rhino we disturbed earlier. Her calf is only a few days old, probably why the mother is nervous."

"You can't possibly know it's the same ones," scoffed Abigail, over the clicking of her phone, as selfie after selfie was taken.

"I know the Rhino here. See how her ear has a notch in it. That's how I recognize her," answered Max. "It's risky for her to come to such an open place, as her baby can be prey to Hyenas and Lions. But with her size and that great horn, she should be able to protect her youngster against all but humans."

"If it doesn't work as medicine, why would they still want it?" asked Dexter.

"Money," replied Max. "It's worth a fortune."

Watching the mother and calf had Abigail fighting back tears; she was such a protective mother and it made her miss her own. Although it had been years since her death, she still had a lingering memory of a faint smell of gardenia, bergamot and rose from her favourite perfume.

"Why'd anyone want to harm them, especially that baby. It is just too cute."

"I know. But some people believe that it can cure all sorts of ailments: from a fever, gout, even cancer."

"Can it?"

"As I said earlier, there is no scientific evidence to support that claim. I think it is more likely to do with money and prestige now."

"What can we do to stop it?" Abigail asked.

All this time Dexter had been listening intently, his head down. He looked up sharply. "You could tell your followers and friends, Abigail."

"A great idea, Dexter. Education is often the key to conservation," said Max.

Looking up again, Dexter noticed a grey shape in the distance. Picking up a pair of binoculars, he scanned the horizon. "Look, another Rhino. But it's hornless."

Picking up his binoculars Max looked in the direction Dexter was pointing.

"Good spotting. We'll make a Ranger out of you yet. Looks like she's with a herd of Wildebeest and Zebra. We often see them all together; the Zebra and Wildebeest help the Rhino with early warning signals."

Beaming under Max's praise, Dexter showed Abigail where to look and passed her the binoculars.

"Awesome. Did a poacher get its horn?"

"Not this time. This Park and several others in Southern Africa have a dehorning programme. This means that they tranquillize them and cut off the horn every few years or so. It grows quite quickly and could be full-size in about three years. It is the only Rhino we've managed to dehorn so far; the costs for this are huge."

"It looks stupid," said Dexter.

"It does—but it might save her life. I flew the chopper when that female was dehorned a month ago. We are still worried that the others we didn't dehorn will be a target—and I'm sure I saw a flash of gunfire the night we flew in."

"The brochure doesn't say anything about us coming to a warzone. If anything happens Daddy will sue," said Abigail.

"Cool. Guns. Just like on the War Zombie game," said Dexter.

For the first time, the trip back to the lodge was filled with the excited chatter from the children who were busy tallying up the creatures that had visited the waterhole: Giraffes with their long necks and long tongues, Sable Antelope with their jet-black coats and sweeping horns, Klipspringer who bounded over the rocks with such ease, Warthogs with their warty faces and funny sticking up tails when they ran, Zebra and Wildebeest that grazed peacefully, and their Rhino sightings.

In the lodge's bar, Theo sat on a stool. He had his head in his hands and a half-drunk glass of whiskey in front of him. When Abigail saw him, she excitedly ran over.

"Daddy. Look! I got new photos. That's sure to boost my followers."

Barely looking up at the excited faces in front of him, Theodore muttered, "Whatever, Princess."

Ntombi: A Rhino's Story

CHAPTER 5

A shout had Ntombi looking up sharply mid-drink, the cool water splashing down her chin. What was that? Glancing towards the rocky granite giants that towered over the waterhole, Ntombi noted her mother barely looked up, continuing to quench her thirst in big gulps. Taking a few steps towards the rock formation to see what was there, she sniffed the air for any strange scents. The granite boulder cast a shadow over the plains below it, its shape stark and silent. Ears twitching for sounds, all that she heard now was the twitter of birds. Ntombi turned back to the water to finish drinking.

The refreshing water had revived Ntombi, and she was looking for something interesting to do. She gave Lindi's tail a tug, and dashed away before her mother could react. It was her favourite game, but Lindi was quiet and still, ignoring her daughter's antics, looking at the setting sun. She called out to the little dusky bird with its fiery beak that sat perched upon her back.

"It will be dark soon. I think it'll be safer with the crash. We will leave at next sun-up. What say you, Izzy?"

"Can't hurt."

"Have you seen the others recently?"

"I think it was some time ago, but I'm sure Tubi and I will be able to help you find them when it is light."

As the pair of Rhino's moved through the African night, grazing on the yellowing grasses that grew on the plains, the two Oxpeckers placed their heads under their wings and fell asleep on the swaying grey backs of their hosts.

Early next morning the "work harder, work

harder" Turtle Dove started his wake-up call, and the cool damp smell faded as the warmth seeped into the earth.

Turning to Ntombi, Lindi gave her calf a nudge. "Right. Let's go find the crash."

"What's the crash, Mama?"

"Our family, little one."

"There are more Lumber-beasts? Yippee."

They set off briskly with Ntombi bounding excitedly alongside Lindi. They walked. And walked. Ntombi started to drop behind, and Lindi had to snort at her to hurry up,

"Are we there yet?"

Sighing, Lindi just continued trudging along.

After they had walked for what seemed like ages, Ntombi was no longer sure exactly where they were going, and the scary hook-beaked rock was just a distant shadow. Ntombi was bouncing around her mother, looking yet again for more mischief, when Lindi stopped abruptly. Ntombi, who wasn't watching where she was going, crashed into her. She peeked around her mother, curious to see why they had stopped.

There in front of Lindi was a moist pile of dung.

She promptly put her nose right on top of it and gave a deep sniff.

Grimacing, Ntombi stared at her mother. "Mama, that's gross."

"Aah good, the crash is not far. These poo-piles are great for sending messages to other Lumber-beasts."

Ntombi was staring intently at the pile. When the pile shifted, she turned her head, moving a little closer. "It moved. The pile moved."

Chuckling, Lindi used her snout to shovel away at the pile, revealing a little inky black Dung Beetle. It was busily raking the pong into a ball with its front arms.

"What is it, Mama?"

"A Chomper."

"Do they eat Poo?"

"I think so."

"Bleuch!"

She sat watching the inky black Dung Beetle as it scraped a pile with its front legs and then moved round and round, over and over until it was a ball. A sly smile crept over Ntombi's face, and she blew hard on the ball.

Phfft.

The Chomper, clinging to his ball frantically, rolled over and over until it came to a stop on its back, feet sticking up in the air. With much effort, he righted himself and moved towards the ball again. Ntombi blew on it again.

Phfft.

"Hehe," she chuckled, as she watched it start the whole process begin again.

"Hey, Tubi! Check this out," called Ntombi as she blew on the creature.

This time Tubi watched gleefully from his vantage point on Ntombi's horn. The two were giggling like monkeys.

"Come, Ntombi," called Lindi.

Listening was not one of Ntombi's strong points and she continued to harass the tiny creature until the poor thing was so dizzy it went round and round in small circles, no longer able to find his dungball.

"NTOMBI! Come on. It's getting late."

"Why? Don't wanna go. Wanna play with the Chompers."

"No. That poo is from a crash member, and they aren't far. Now leave it alone."

With the two flappers flying in front, Lindi and Ntombi followed them briskly, eager to get to the crash before it was too late, and they had moved on to the chomping grounds.

"Not far now, Ntombi. I see them ahead."

Ntombi gave a squeak and broke into an excited trot.

"Wait, Ntombi. Don't rush."

Slowly her mother approached the shade-givers and there, gathered underneath, were Lumber-beasts of all sizes.

"Eeek, Eeek!" squeaked Lindi.

A bulky crinkly lumbering Rhino slowly shuffled towards them.

Bowing her head, Lindi moved forward to respectfully touch noses with the older beast. "Ntombi, this is Gogo."

Staring at the impressive bulk of Gogo who looked down at the tiny Rhino, Ntombi shuffled her round feet in the dirt. Nudging her daughter, Lindi gently pushed her in the direction of the Rhino's matriarch.

"Say Hello, Ntombi."

Stumbling a little, Ntombi just managed to mumble.

"Hi," she said shyly.

Gogo smiled kindly and gave her a little wink, crinkling her already wrinkled face even further.

"Yebo, little one. Back so soon, Lindi? Didn't expect you back with us for another few weeks."

"Aye, I know Gogo. But those uprights with their death-spitting sticks were hunting me. Safer here. With you."

"Maiwe. Are we never to be free?" Gogo shook her head. "But come now, let's show the little girly her family."

Ntombi lost track of all the snouts she touched and was feeling a little overwhelmed when another young Rhino stepped in front of her.

"Howzit, I'm Balega. Wanna play?"

Ntombi looked to her mother.

Lindi nodded, moving off to chat with Gogo, and Balega's mother, Sisi.

Off raced the two new friends, round and round where Gogo and Lindi were lying in the shade-giver.

"Cut that out, you two. It's making too much dust," grumbled one of the others.

The naughty pair simply ignored the complaints, until they collapsed together giggling.

"Ntombi, have you heard about Swazi?" asked Balega.

"No, what's a Swazi?"

"Not a what, a who. He is the oldest and biggest of all the Lumber-beasts. Mother says he has a horn that is as high as the top of that shade-giver."

Ntombi looked at the shade-giver then at Balega, "No way! Where is he then?"

"Dunno. Mother says he flits about the territory. Not everyone has seen him. I asked Fumbɪ—he is older than us and he knows lots of stuff. He says that Swazi is the biggest Lumber-beast he has ever seen. He says that Swazi even fought off a group of Death-Uprights."

"Balega, what are Death-Uprights?"

"Oh, you know those scary Upright walking things."

"Oh, I've seen some of those. They look like fun."

"My Mama says they are dangerous."

"Why?"

Pleased that he knew more than Ntombi, Balega puffed his chest out as he boasted, "Don't you know anything? They have BIG sticks that spit-death."

Pondering this conversation, Ntombi looked at Lindi and then at Gogo.

Lindi had a nice tall but rounded horn, but Gogo's was completely gone. Her face had a flat disk, and you could see a dark heart where it had been sheered right off. Where was Gogo's horn? Ntombi was puzzled. Did Gogo survive the 'Death-Uprights'?

The shade had all but gone and the whiny Cicadas grew louder still. As was their normal custom, the Lumber-beasts were spread out under the bushes that provided the best shade, avoiding the rising heat. As the matriarch, Gogo lay snoozing under the lushest, greenest, and tallest shrub on the savannah, the others making do with the sparse shelter they could find.

Still pondering Gogo's lost horn, Ntombi lay next to Lindi, and Balega's mother, Sisi. She tossed and turned, huffed, and puffed.

Fed up Lindi turned and scolded her daughter. "Oh Ntombi. Stop that fidgeting!"

So Ntombi wandered over to Balega, as he was a bit older, and he never let her forget it. He was sure to know.

"Balega! Why doesn't Gogo have a horn?"

Swishing his tail lazily at a persistent Fly, Balega opened one eye and gave a shrug. "Uhh, dunno."

"Come. Let's ask her."

With another shrug, Balega gave a yawn as his eye slid closed. "Too hot."

Kicking dust in his face, Ntombi stomped off. "Fine. I'll ask Gogo."

"Just what are you going to ask Gogo?"

Lindi raised her head.

"About her missing horn."

Shaking her head sadly, Lindi lowered her voice and whispered, "Ag, Ntombi. Don't ask Gogo that."

"Why not?"

"Gogo might be upset that she doesn't have one."

"Why'd she be upset?"

"Ntombi, you're too young to understand."

Ignoring her mother, Ntombi bound up to Gogo who lay under her dense thick shade-giver.

"Gogo! Where's your horn?"

From her spot underneath a less shady thorn bush, Lindi's raised voice could be heard.

"Ntombi, I told you not to bother Gogo."

"But it's a good story, Lindi."

"Ntombi is too little, Gogo."

"No, no, it's good that she learns this. Sit. Sit. You too, Balega and Tubi."

Gogo arranged herself comfortably in the shade in front of her eager audience, clearing her throat. "Some time ago, I was peacefully snoozing, avoiding the hottest time, when one of those smelly, noisy Clatter bang things—"

"What's a clatter-bang?" interrupted Ntombi.

With a huge sigh, Balega rolled his eyes and shoved Ntombi with his small horn. Surely every Rhino knew that clattering trucks carried tourists into the park.

"Those funny things that give birth to the Uprights. Now shush."

Nodding at Balega, Gogo continued.

"Eh-eh. Well, this Clatter-bang erupted out of the bushes filled with Uprights all in green like the colour of some shade-givers."

Pausing dramatically, Gogo made sure that her audience was captivated. The two Rhino calves and the flapper were looking at her in awe.

Satisfied, Gogo nodded and continued, "Up above a strange flapper flew without flapping— Whop, Whop—the sound it made was deafening. Eh, I tell you. My heart was pounding. I leapt up trying to find a way to escape but the Uprights were all over. Everywhere."

"What happened next, Gogo?" Balega and Ntombi asked eagerly.

Gazing into the distance, Gogo murmured absentmindedly.

"Hmmmm!"

The two squeaked impatiently and Tubi who was perched on Gogo's horn gave a little chirp.

"What happened?"

"Huh! Then, I felt a sharp prick on my bottom, worse than any Bite-yous. I was terrified, I tell you. I tried to run but the legs didn't work too good. I crashed to the floor, fast asleep. When I woke, my beautiful horn was gone."

Staring in amazement at Gogo, Balega's eyes widened at the thought of a vanishing horn. "It was gone. Where?"

"Angazi."

Beating Ntombi to the question, Tubi interrupted, "Who's Angazi?"

"It means that I don't know, it's an expression."

Stamping one of his large round feet, Balega impatiently scolded Tubi. "Let Gogo finish, Tubi."

"You know, that Swazi, he is too clever."

Two heads swivelled around in shock, Balega's eyes widened when he heard this. "You know Swazi, Gogo?"

"Eh-eh. We were together. I tell you; he was too clever. He escaped. I haven't seen him since."

Giving a great sigh, Gogo continued.

"Ag, I shall miss my horn, but it'll grow back."

"Grow back, Gogo?" Ntombi asked, puzzled.

"Yes, little one. Our horns keep growing, all our lives."

His head on his knees, Balega stared at Gogo.

As if seeing her properly for the first time, he spoke quietly, "Gogo? Did the Uprights with the death-spitting sticks take your horn?"

"I doubt it. I would not be here if they did."

Puzzled, Ntombi looked at Gogo.

"Why? Where would you be?"

"Travelling with the wind. Gone."

The calves looked at Gogo, they had never heard their mothers speak this way. Looking up sharply from her nap, Lindi cut in hurriedly.

"That's enough, Gogo. They are too young for such talk."

Stamping her foot, Ntombi pouted at her mother.

"But Mama, I wanna know how Gogo will fly."

"I said enough. Now run along and play."

Huffing, Ntombi stamped her foot again.

"But I'm big, Mama," argued Ntombi.

"Enough, Ntombi. I'm sure that Sisi wouldn't want Balega to know such things either."

Lindi looked towards the shade-giver where Sisi lay, her great head resting comfortably on her front feet. Only a couple of toes peeked out from under her chin.

"Okay," mumbled Ntombi, and she stomped off with Balega behind her. Tubi flew to a nearby tree and busied himself with preening, his bright red and yellow beak stroking his dusky-brown feathers.

"I is big enough, Balega. Not a baby," said Ntombi, "It's not fair."

"You're IT," yelled Balega. He nudged her with his stumpy horn and turned to speed away.

The next minute a piercing shriek interrupted their game as a screaming ball of fur exploded from a crop of rocky giants. Its scruffy brindled fur, sticky-out ears and piercing orange eyes darted over its shoulder as it ran. A long thin tail followed it and seemed to have a mind of its own; it went up, and then changed its mind and went downwards.

Chirping and squawking, Tubi flapped about in alarm as the screaming continued.

"Tsk, Kirr."

"He's after me, he's after me."

Spinning round in a cloud of dust, Ntombi snorted, looking for her mother, whose head was raised, ears swivelling, trying to find the source of all the noise. The screaming continued and more balls of fur were bursting through the bush all making a terrible fracas. Screaming and squealing, dust and fur flying everywhere—it was as if the savannah was suddenly surrounded by these creatures, as their grunts, groans and chattering could be heard in stereo.

As her daughter skidded around behind her, puffing hard, Lindi spotted the source of all the noise; a small Baboon, who was taking advantage of the two large grey Rhino and had slid in-between Ntombi's legs.

"Mama! Get it away from me."

Looking round to see the little pink face peer out from between Ntombi's front legs, Lindi grunted, "It's just a silly Wahu." And she returned to her snoozing.

What odd-looking beasts, thought Ntombi, looking at the original fur ball, who came screeching up to Ntombi and hid between her thick grey legs.

Peering out of its hiding place, its tail tickling Ntombi's tummy, it asked, "Has he gone?"

Now that the noise seemed to have died down, Tubi landed on Ntombi's horn and Balega ran over to see the curious creature.

She came out from between Ntombi's legs, grinning, showing her pink gums and sharp teeth. "Phew! That was close. Howzit? I'm Jabu."

"I'm Ntombi. This is Tubi and that's Balega. What's up?"

Grinning cheekily, opening his long thin finger, she held up a small purple-red fruit. "A spat with my big brother, I stole his fruit."

"Why so much noise?" said Ntombi.

"It's the way we keep track of everyone in our troop." More and more of the fuzzy, noisy creatures emerged from the trees and rocky crevices as if by magic, grunting and groaning as they scratched through the dust and poo piles, and picked the fruit from the trees around them.

"What's a troop?"

"Our family."

Through a mouthful of swishy grass, only half-listening to the conversation Balega mumbled, "Oh, ours is called a crash."

"Ja, I know. Ndoda is the boss and the biggest. He's also the grouchiest and bites if you annoy him. I try to stay out of his way."

They looked over at Ndoda who sat perched on a large granite boulder, his long thin hands dangling over his knees. As they watched, he opened his mouth to yawn, exposing his massive sharp pointed teeth.

Eyes widening, Tubi gasped. "Ouch. I see why he's the boss."

"I think Gogo is our Leader; Mama & Sisi listen to her. She is very wise," said Ntombi.

All the time they were talking, Jabu was busy scratching through a poo-pile.

Watching Jabu, Ntombi scrunched up her nose. "What are you doing with that? It's GROSS?"

"Looking for Chompers and seeds to eat. Yummmm. Want one?"

Smacking her lips together, she held up a small wriggling black Beetle.

"No thanks. Yuck. I drink from my Mama and sometimes eat swishy-snack."

"What's a swishy-snack?"

Lifting his head, a grassy swishy-snack poking out of his mouth, Balega looked at Jabu in amazement. "The tall stuff that grows straight up and swishes about in the breeze."

Perched on Ntombi's head, Tubi had other ideas as he looked at the thick fur covering Jabu's thin body.

"Do you have any Bite-yous?"

Shaking her head, Jabu pointed towards a group that sat under the shade of a small grey thorn tree. "Nah, Mama insists on cleaning me, so embarrassing. Look."

The others looked in the direction Jabu was pointing to see a baby Baboon being cleaned by its mother. The mother was picking and nibbling at its fur whilst the baby wriggled, trying to get free, squealing like a little pig.

With a sudden thought, Balega brightened. "Jabu, did you say you wanted Poo-Chompers? I know a place where you can get some."

"You do? Where?"

So, the four of them wandered off towards a pile of poo and Jabu eagerly attacked the pile with gusto. Bits of half chewed grass and the odd seed flung about as she searched for her prize.

The two Lumber-beasts and Tubi sat under a nearby shade-giver, Tubi hopping from ear to ear, looking for his favourite snack of Bite-yous.

Still thinking about Gogo's story, Ntombi turned to Balega, who was watching Jabu with disgust.

"I don't know why Mama wouldn't let Gogo finish her story. So unfair."

"My mama would have told us."

Catching the tail end of their conversation, Jabu wandered over. Tiny bits of half-chewed Beetle landed on Ntombi's head as she spoke, "Whaths thstory?"

Leaping back to avoid the barrage of Beetle spit, Ntombi rubbed her head on a nearby tree.

"Eeew. Stop that Jabu."

Holding a shiny black Beetle in his long thin fingers, Jabu ignored Ntombi's disgust and boasted, "I know what happens."

Cocking his head to the side, Balega looked at the scruffy Baboon sceptically. "No. You don't."

"I do. I promise you. My mama told me."

"Well, tell us then, Jabu," said Ntombi.

Finishing off his meal, Jabu sat up and placed her hands on her knees, just like she had seen the leader of her troop, Ndoda, do.

"Well. Those bug-eyed noisy shiny flappers chase you, then with a magical zap from a pointy stick. *Thwack.* They get you and you fall fast asleep."

"No way," said Ntombi.

"No! They don't," retorted Balega. "You're a liar."

"Na, it's true. Then that metal flapper lands and Uprights run like ants and steal your horn whilst you are in sleepy land," said Jabu.

"You're making it up."

"I'm not. Ask Tubi. He knows too."

"Hey!" responded Tubi, "I'm not telling. Lindi will stomp on me for sure. I've already been sat on by a Lumber-beast. Don't wish to repeat that experience."

"Well, don't go under my tail and I won't sit on you," said Ntombi, flicking her tail.

"Tell us, Tubi," encouraged Balega. "We won't tell. Honest."

Ruffling his feathers, Tubi shook his head vigorously. "Nuh-uh, not worth it. Ask your new friend Jabu, she seems to have loose lips."

"Come on. Tell us, Jabu. I'll show you another Pongy Poo pile. Full of these delicious Chompers. Won't we, Balega?" urged Ntombi.

"More Chompers. Alright I'll tell ya," agreed Jabu, popping another black Beetle into her mouth. "There's a place on the other side of the strange silver boundary. It's not a safe place."

Crunch, went the next Beetle, and another. Jabu licked her fingers one by one before continuing. "We were spread out all looking for tasty titbits when Mama and I saw two or three like you. Bigs ones they were, except their life force had long passed, and they lay there still and unmoving. And where their horns should have been was a huge gaping hole. It was too terrible."

Then came a short bark.

"I have to go."

And with that Jabu bound through the grass and clambered onto the back of her mother. She looked back at the trio of friends with a cheeky grin and a wave.

"Check ya, guys."

And with that, they were gone.

The shocked friends sat there, stunned by what Jabu had told them.

A shudder racked through Ntombi. "I want my Mama," she said.

Ntombi rushed over to her mother and nuzzled into Lindi's side, looking for her sweet, warm comforting milk.

Ntombi: A Rhino's Story

CHAPTER 6

Shortly after meeting Jabu, the cheeky and scruffy Baboon, the young Rhino Ntombi came across some of the strangest beasts she had ever seen. First, there was a bunch of stripy looking beasts, at least she thought they were a bunch. All the stripes mingled when they moved, tails flicking back and forth as Flies hummed about them. Every so often one of them would stamp a hoofed foot to get rid of the biting Flies. Scattered amongst the Zebra were a group of shaggy looking beasts, a jumble of ears, horns, and knobbly knees. The strange-looking Wildebeest looked as if they had been made up of spare parts.

The three friends stood staring at these funny creatures wondering what they could be.

Cocking her head to the side, Ntombi watched the Zebra as they moved, a wave of black and white stripes. "What are those?"

Looking up from his snacking, Balega gave a gasp. "Are they eating our Swishy-snack?"

"What do you think, Tubi? Have you seen these before?"

Tubi didn't even get a chance to reply, before one shaggy Wildebeest suddenly bolted in their direction. The two Lumber-beasts looked around for their mothers, ready to take off if given the go ahead.

"Gnee, Gnu, Gnee, Gnu," said the knobbly-kneed Wildebeest.

Nervously, Ntombi and Balega backed away from this weird looking beast, when it came to a shuddering halt in front of them.

Swallowing a gulp, Balega muttered, "Boy, that thing's weird."

He stared at its sticky out horns, large vacant

eyes and sparse shaggy hair that sprouted out of its chin and back. It had the knobbiest knees too, looking as if it had been put together in a hurry. Sniffing at the Wildebeest, Ntombi looked nervously about for her mother.

"Hhhhello!"

"Gnu."

"What's your name?" said Balega.

"Gnee."

Startled at the answer, Ntombi giggled.

With a twitter, Tubi hopped towards the end of Ntombi's snout.

"Pleased to meet you, Gnee?"

"Gnu, Gnee."

A snort erupted from Ntombi, and she firmly placed her lips together trying to stifle another giggle, as Balega bravely took a step towards it.

"Perhaps they speak another language."

Raising his voice, Balega said slowly, "HELLO, WHAT'S YOUR NAME?"

"GNEE."

"W-H-A-T'S Y-O-U-R N-A-M-E?" The three of them shouted. Perhaps if they spoke louder, he would understand.

With a little flutter, Tubi flew from Ntombi and landed on the Wildebeests' head. He was certain he had spotted a tasty Tick.

The skittish creature leapt into the air, flicking out his back hooves.

"Gnu."

Off it darted again, zigzagging away in a spray of dust.

Ntombi and Balega stared at each other in bewilderment.

Noticing the two young Rhinos' confusion, Tubi chirped up. "It's a Shaggy beast. It has good Bite-yous."

Next, the young duo turned their curious looks to the other creature on the plains that day, the stripy ones. They were rather striking and far less alarming looking. They noticed that there was a smaller one amongst them, and after a lengthy discussion, decided to see if it was friendly.

They casually ambled towards it and what they assumed was its mother, stopping every few feet to scent the air as their mothers had taught them to do.

Finally, they stopped a few meters in front of the little stripy creature.

"Hi," they said in unison.

The little stripey Zebra looked up with large dark eyes.

"Hello. What are you?"

"What are we? What are you?"

"I'm Dube," it said proudly. "I'm a stripy beast."

"I'm Balega, and this is Ntombi. We are Lumber-beasts; the biggest of all the beasts here," said Balega boastfully.

Tubi leapt around on Ntombi's back not wanting to be left out. "I'm a flapper called Tubi," he said.

"Nice to meet you. Look at me." Dube took off at speed, dashing through the trees.

"Wow!" said Ntombi and Balega together.

"He sure is fast," said Balega, in awe.

"I do wish he would stop; he is making my eyes go funny," added Ntombi, as the stripes blurred in front of her.

Dube came running back to them in a blur of stripes and stopped in a cloud of dust.

"I'm fast, hey?" Dube said with a neigh. "What can you do?"

"Um, I already said. We are the biggest."

"And Gogo says that we will grow nice big horns," added Balega, as an afterthought.

"Big ones like Swazi."

"Cool! I've got to go. Byeeee!"

Racing off, their new stripy friend joined the rest of the Zebra herd, melting into the shadows of the trees. Looking at each other, Ntombi and Balega shrugged and carried on with their snacking.

They hardly had their heads down when Tubi, Izzy and the other Oxpeckers flew up into the air, shrieking their alarm call. Both Ntombi and Balega looked around for their mothers, something horrible was coming.

"Mama!" Ntombi called.

A cloud of dust was charging in their direction. As it came closer, the strange shaggy beasts darted around them, the whites of their eyes visible in their panic.

Next came Dube and his herd. "Jijima," he shouted, as he ran towards them.

"What?" shouted Ntombi.

"Run, Ntombi, Run," shouted Dube again, his eyes wild as he galloped away.

Then Ntombi and Balega saw it. The battered helicopter thundered towards them, its windscreen looking like large eyes glinting in the sunlight, its great shadow blocking out the sun.

Terrified, Ntombi and Balega turned and raced back to their mothers, who were looking frantically for their babies. Appearing next to the calves, Gogo snorted and pushed each youngster in turn as the mothers raced to protect their babies.

"Run. The Flapper that steals horns."

The helicopter hovered above them, its blades creating a gush of wind and swirling a multitude of russet-coloured leaves high into the sky. From a gaping door on its side, the outline of a human and a deadly rifle pointing in their direction could be seen.

Then Lindi turned and pushed Ntombi in front of her. They fled from the open plains and into the hidden valleys of the nearby granite giants, the rest of the crash following them.

The whomping blades of the helicopter could be heard as they echoed through the hills of the Dwala Safari Park.

Whomp, Whomp.

On the other side of the small crop of rocks, the human in the helicopter waited for the Rhinos, rifle poised for a clear shot when they emerged. They gave up when the Rhino stayed hidden, and the pilot spotted a cherry red helicopter on the horizon. They turned hastily away towards the sun, its brightness camouflaging them and enabling them to escape without being spotted by the other chopper. It fled, knowing that it was only a matter of time before they got another chance at the Rhino and their valuable horns.

Watching from the valley, Gogo breathed a sigh of relief as the helicopter left. She cautiously walked back into the open plains, the others following her lead. They had no sooner stepped out into the open when the other helicopter was upon them, and panting they zigzagged back through the trees to the safety of their hiding place. Overcome with curiosity, Ntombi turned back to get a better look.

Lindi spun around looking for her daughter. "Ntombi! Get back here! Now!"

The tone of her mother's voice made Ntombi turn reluctantly into the shadows provided by the granite rocks.

With a sigh, Lindi pushed her behind Balega. "Maiwe! You are going to be the death of me for sure."

The helicopter blades sliced through the warm midday air, making the trees sway against the strength of the wind.

Max had convinced them to take a chopper ride over the Safari Park. It was a great way to see wildlife and a quick way to check up on the fences. Besides, he was still a little worried about the gunfire that he had seen on their arrival.

As she looked down on the parched landscape below, Abigail thought how different it all looked from the air, especially during the day. As she watched the shadow of their helicopter undulating over the plains and the balancing

103

boulders below, she saw a herd of Zebra with several Wildebeest, galloping at full tilt, zipping through the sparse Acacia scrub and Terminalia trees. "Hey! Look! I see something!"

Looking down, Max saw what had gotten Abigail so excited. He gave a shout through the headphones. "Great spotting, Abi. Looks like a herd of Zebra and Wildebeest. They are often seen together. Safety in numbers."

He turned the chopper in the direction of the herd and as he did the Wildebeest ran from the whomp of the cherry-coloured helicopter, skipping helter-skelter over the open plain. Leaving chaos in their wake, Zebra and Wildebeest ran in all directions, and then just in front of them, they saw large grey shapes, probably six or seven.

Peering through the window, his face leaving a smudge on the window and his Nintendo momentarily forgotten, Dexter spotted the shapes. From above they looked a little like the boulders that dotted through the plains until the boulder ran.

"What are those?"

"Rhino. A whole herd, although they are sometimes referred to as a crash of Rhino."

Leaning in her seat and pressing her phone to the window, Abigail had her finger on the shutter, as the camera on the phone clicked away. "Get closer, Max. I want a close-up."

At the mention of the Rhino, Theo suddenly glanced up from his phone. "Get closer, I wanna see the size of their horns."

Shaking his head, Max turned the chopper in the opposite direction when he saw the Rhinos run in a panic, the mothers pushing their young calves in front of them. "They're very skittish. Best we head back."

Later, after a hot and sweaty helicopter flight, they were all sipping cool refreshing drinks in the lounge area. The tan leather chairs felt cool against their backs, as the fans hummed and squeaked from the dark wooden beams of the thatched roof.

"Max, look! It's that hornless Rhino again. And there are some babies. Oh, that one is so cute. So curious."

Taking the phone from Abigail, Max looked at the slightly out-of-focus image on the screen.

"I'm impressed that you managed to get these photos, Abi."

Scrolling through the other images that Abigail had managed to capture, Max noted how dry and barren the land was looking. He handed the phone back to the girl. "I'm worried that the Rhino will have no water soon. The Park is very dry. From the looks of your photos, Abi, the only water around is on the other side of the park boundary."

"Surely they can just drink there then."

"It's not safe for them outside the park. It has been referred to as poachers' corner."

"It's fenced, isn't it?"

"It is fenced, but the park doesn't have enough money to keep repairing the fences. Poachers often cut them and start a fire to push the animals out."

Dumping his Nintendo on the table in front of him with a thump, Dexter peered over Max's shoulder. "Why did you only dehorn that one?"

"Some of the Rhinos were too young to be dehorned. We normally wait until they are a few years old. There were a few pregnant ones, and we leave them alone as there may be issues with the drugs we use to put them to sleep. There was a bull with that old female, but he managed to get away before we could dart him. The dehorning programme is very expensive, so it's only done every few years."

Losing interest, Dexter flopped back down in his chair and continued playing on his console.

"Dexter, is that blasted thing attached to your arm?" said Max.

Barely looking up, Dexter mumbled over the shooting sounds coming from the Nintendo. "It's a new game, shooting Zombies from a helicopter. It's way cool. At Level 7, I get a bigger gun."

A loud jangle came from Theodore's pocket. He was snoozing in the comfy brown leather armchair; jerked suddenly awake he fumbled for his phone, "HELLO?"

Hearing her father's voice, Abigail turned and shoved her phone under his nose. "Daddy, look I got a great photo. Should I post it?"

Theo glanced briefly at his daughter's phone, noticing the slightly blurry image of a hornless

Rhino, and shoved Abigail's hand out of the way.

"But Daddy. Looook." Her lip quivered.

"Oh, for heaven's sake Abigail. It doesn't have a horn. Not even a proper Rhino. Show me one with a horn."

Max shrugged apologetically at the other guests, who had looked in their direction again at the sound of Theo's raised voice. Turning towards Abigail, he heard the distinctive ping of her phone that signalled a post being "liked".

"Did you do as I asked and switch your mobile to flight mode?"

"Yeah, yeah."

Flicking her hand dismissively in Max's direction, Abigail watched as the "likes" came rolling in. She got off her chair and wandered towards the swimming pool. "A thousand likes already," said Abie over her shoulder, diving into the pool.

Shrugging, Dexter followed.

CHAPTER 7

The earth was sizzling. Hazy heat shimmered up across the parched landscape of the Dwala Safari Park. The hum and whine of the noisy Cicadas were deafening; the hotter it got, the louder the bugs seemed to get. Red dust rose and swirled. In the distance, a trail of dust plumed behind a clatter-bang, carrying yet another batch of Uprights.

For once Ntombi lay still, resting with her mother, under the sparse shade. The shade-givers leaves had long since dropped to the ground leaving nothing but a few bare sticks. The rest of the crash were scattered nearby, all trying to find the best shade. Even Gogo's special shade-giver was bald.

The flappers all sat on the backs of their chosen Lumber-beast, their beaks open, as they panted in the heat.

"I'm thirsty, Mama," said Ntombi.

"Later, we'll go to the water hole, little one."

The hot ball was sinking into the earth, when the Lumber-beasts ambled to the water hole, crunching, and crashing through the shrivelled vegetation of the territory, their large round feet stirring clouds of dust. The hook-snout shaped boulder with the scowl permanently etched into his granite face looked grimly down on the sepia landscape.

Hidden in its crevasses stood two humans all in green, rifles slung across their shoulders silently guarding the Rhino.

"Where is it?" said Balega. "Where's it gone?"

In front of them—where the waterhole used to be—was a dehydrated, cracked, and withered patch of rusty earth, only slight dampness left at

110

the very centre. Looking at the patch, Gogo nodded at the other older beasts and turned to lead them away.

With a sigh, Lindi circled behind Ntombi and gave her a gentle push. "Come on, little one."

"I don't wanna walk. I want water."

"We will go to another waterhole. Don't worry little one. Have a suckle first, then we will go."

Patiently, Lindi waited for Ntombi to finish slurping before she got up, forcing Ntombi to follow her.

In a blink, the light was gone, and it turned into glittering inky darkness. They trudged onto the next waterhole, but it too was drained. So was the next.

Standing at the edge of the dried cracked mud where the water hole use to be, Gogo sniffed sadly. "Aiy. This is too terrible. We must go to Demoni waterhole."

Shocked Lindi shook her head vigorously. "No! It's too dangerous."

"What's dangerous?" said Balega, his swivel ears picking up the adult's conversation.

Ignoring Balega, Gogo sighed. "We have no choice."

Brightening a little, Lindi had a thought. "What about the Valley waterhole?"

"Aiy. No. That grumpy bull Lumber-beast is too cheeky."

Shuddering, Sisi remembered her last run in with the territorial black Rhino who had come boiling out from the shadow, snorting, and puffing.

With another sniff Gogo, looked at the two worried mothers, knowing that Valley waterhole was not an option either.

"Gone. Just a puddle. Farai, she told me."

Sitting down with a thump, Sisi allowed Balega to nuzzle for a drink. "Maiwe, we must go to Demoni. But what if it is dry too?"

"We have to try," said Gogo.

Shaking uncontrollably, Lindi collapsed next to Sisi, as memories of the last time she had been at that dreadful place flooded her head; had she not smelt the tell-tale sign of the approaching dangers, Ntombi might never have been born.

"NO! There is danger there. I barely escaped last time."

Watching the adults with interest, Ntombi bounced in front of Gogo. "What is the Demoni?"

"It is a terrible place. Most who go there do not come back. There was this Lumber-beast I once knew—"

"NO! Do not fill these babies' heads with such things."

Moving in between the matriarch and the two calves, Sisi and Lindi shook their heads vigorously at Gogo. The two youngsters looked on, shocked at their meek mothers standing up to Gogo. Milk dribbled down Balega's chin, his mother had stood up so quickly that it had interrupted his drink.

"Okay. We go to Demoni, but you Mama's find a place to rest with these little ones."

With that, Gogo gathered the other adult members of the Rhino crash, leaving the mothers to settle their offspring.

Throughout the night the mothers moved from clump to clump of swishy-snack, whispering furtively to each other.

"I hope they find something soon, Sisi," said Lindi.

"Or it falls from above," said Sisi, looking upward, hopefully, as the shadows of the seemingly endless night lightened and the bush around them came alive with the calls of birds. Already they could feel the hot dry rays as it prepared to continue its assault on the earth.

Gogo and the others did not return that day, so the mothers and their calves stayed close together, grazing on what little there was to eat and resting during the hottest hours.

On the horizon, a strange darkness loomed, and an eerie quietness clung to the granite giants. A strange damp smell was carried on the breeze. Ntombi lifted her snout towards the smell, it smelt cool and wet and welcoming. Suddenly, the sun was obscured by the heavy indigo clouds.

"Balega, where's the warm ball gone?"

"Dunno. Too hot."

Shrugging, Ntombi placed her head on her knees. Balega was right—it was too hot to be curious.

A bright flash of light lit up the sky with a jagged crack as if the sky was being split in two; followed by a loud angry growl. With a jolt, Ntombi woke from her dream of cool sweet liquid running down her throat. Another flash, then—CRASH. Bang. Crack.

Up leapt Ntombi and Balega, causing a snoozing Tubi to flap about in alarm.

"MAMA!"

Nuzzling her terrified little one, who was busy burying her head in her mother's side, Lindi said comfortingly, "It's okay little one. The wet-stuff is coming."

Casually sauntering away from his own mother, Balega scoffed. "You see. It's nothing. You big baby."

"I'm not a baby, Balega. Besides you were scared too."

"No. I wasn't."

"Yes, you were."

Seeing his friends wide square bottom lip beginning to quiver, Tubi leapt to Ntombi's defence and gave Balega a quick peck on his nose before flapping off.

"Stop being mean to Ntombi."

Plip, plop, plip, plop.

Droplets fell slowly at first, getting faster and faster, harder, and harder. More flashes and Bang-crashes. *Plip, plop, plippity, plop.* Faster and faster, harder and harder, until it was a sheet of water

115

falling thick and fast from above.

Ntombi stood, enthralled. She breathed it in. Oh! The smell! The intoxicating earthy, musty, sweet smell. Cooling streams of wet-stuff flooded her hot, grey wrinkled skin. Ntombi leapt about joyfully and rushed over to Lindi in excitement.

"Come, Ntombi. Drink first."

The rain continued to pelt down on the parched landscape, creating gushing rivers and turning the dry dusty ground into splishy puddles. It gradually began to ebb and then stopped altogether.

A slow smile crept over Ntombi's face as she spotted a gigantic slushy puddle. She looked at Balega, and they ran. Skidding and sliding across the sodden earth, they leapt into the puddle together, tumbling in with a huge squelchy *SPLASH*.

"Ooooh, this is amazing!"

Leaping into yet another puddle, Ntombi proceeded to roll in it completely until all you could see were her feet sticking up in the air, Balega not far behind her.

Laughing at her daughter, Lindi plopped herself down and giggled when the mud oozed between her toes. With a satisfied sigh Lindi lay down, feeling the cooling mud seep into her thick wrinkly skin.

Watching this, Ntombi giggled; her mother looked so carefree. "You look silly, Mama. Why is there not more wet-stuff?"

From out of nowhere, Gogo and the others appeared, pushing their way through the bush; the thorny branches scraping against their sides as they sloshed through the puddles at their feet.

"It comes when it comes. Sometimes it's wet and sometimes it's dry," said Gogo.

From the ground came a little chirp from Tubi who had been enjoying a refreshing puddle bath. Being an Oxpecker was dirty work. "Gogo! You're back!"

"Gogo, did you get to Demoni?" said Lindi.

Easing her colossal behind into the nearest puddle, the mud sloshed over Gogo's side like a mini tidal wave. "We turned back when the wet-stuff fell. We are saved."

The sounds of splashing and squelching could be heard coming from all the Rhino, bits of mud sent flying as they rolled about in the sludge.

Balega was leaping about from puddle to puddle, yelling as he raced off. "Come catch me, Ntombi,"

Taking off after him, Ntombi's earlier complaints of the heat were a distant memory.

Later, mother and daughter lay side-by-side drying their bodies. The others had wandered off to better chomping grounds nearby.

"Aah," they sighed in unison.

Lindi eventually roused herself and clambered to her feet, waking Ntombi in the process.

"Let's go to the scratcher, little one."

"Scratcher? What's that, Mama?" asked Ntombi dozily.

With a mysterious smile, Lindi lumbered away, calling over her shoulder, "You'll see."

Not long after, they came to a clearing amongst the Shade-givers. There in the middle stood a smooth old broken stump, rubbed this way by continuous Lumber-beast use.

Ntombi stared at it. "Is that it? What does it do?"

"Come, Ntombi," called Lindi, after she had given it a sniff.

118

To Ntombi's amazement, Lindi turned around. Placing her enormous bottom on the scratcher, she started to rub. *Scratchity-scratch* went Lindi, a blissful smile on her face. On and on she went, scratching her rump and her side and under her belly, creating little dust clouds, as she rubbed away the dried mud.

"Ha-ha, Mama, you are too funny," chortled Ntombi.

"Your turn."

Ntombi walked over to the post and copied Lindi.

"This is soooo good."

"Always do this after a mud bath; it helps to get rid of Bite-yous."

On hearing this, Tubi's coffee-coloured head popped out from under Ntombi's stomach, a blueish-grey Tick wriggling in his beak. "Hey! But that's my job."

"Sorry, Tubi. Sometimes we Lumber-beasts get more Bite-yous than you can eat."

Smacking his red-yellow beak as he flung the Tick into the air and caught it with a snap, gulping it down.

"Why's this blasted place so hot?" said Theo, wiping a hand across his sweaty reddened forehead.

It was mid-morning and already the sweltering heat shimmered across the plains as if the sun was trying suck every bit of moisture from an already parched earth. Large white fluffy clouds drifted across the sky.

Sitting in the back of the truck, Abigail and Dexter waved both their arms frantically, as the Mopane Flies hummed around their faces every time the vehicle stopped.

Sweat trickled down Abi's face leaving a streak of mascara and base behind it. "It's been over an hour, and we haven't seen anything. Let's go back."

Max brought the safari truck to a stop against a crop of granite rocks. The boulders created a little shade as they balanced on top of one another. "Let's stop for a drink and then to the last waterhole before heading back."

Taking the offered drink, Dexter gulped it down before whining, "But all the other waterholes have been dry and had no animals."

It was true. The waterholes had all shrunk to nothing but dry cracked puddles and, so far, the wildlife had been scarce. Knowing that most animals would have risen earlier, Max had talked to them at dinner the previous evening about the virtues of an early morning game drive to catch the more nocturnal creatures, as well as to avoid the hottest time of the day. Even so, he had waited that morning for his guests to arrive until the camp staff were just about to start clearing the remnants of breakfast to begin preparations for lunch. As a result, it was already quite warm by the time they left, and they had seen little, except for a few Baboons and the odd Wildebeest.

With a huff, Theo snatched an icy drink from the cooler box in the back of the truck, downing it in one gulp. He chucked the empty tin can over his shoulder and into the bush behind him.

Noticing this, Max hastily hurried to retrieve it and returned the can to a box in the back of the truck, to be correctly disposed of at camp. After his guests had downed more cold drinks, Max packed the cooler into the vehicle.

"Right. Let's get to that waterhole then."

"Listen, driver. It's too hot. I'm not paying to be hot."

"Max. Please call me Max."

"Whatever. Take us back to the lodge. The travel agent will hear about this."

"Fine. Let's head back then."

They hadn't gone far when a strong wind blew across the plains, carrying an earthy petrichor smell. Dark indigo clouds rolled in, blotting out the sun. On the horizon, the slashing grey sheets of rain were visible against the dark clouds.

Stopping, Max breathed in the smell before turning to all his guests. "The rains are coming."

No sooner had he said that than a rumble of thunder echoed through the granite hills. It ended in a crashing crescendo about them, followed by a blinding flash of lightning.

Shouting to be heard above the roar of thunder and rain, Max leapt from the driver's seat of the open-backed truck. "Do you want me to put the rain covers down?"

It was too late. The downpour hit them, and Max was drenched in a matter of minutes.

Whilst Max struggled with the canvas straps on the Land Rovers' roof, Theo looked about in a panic and tried to shove his expensive phone into the console of the truck. "Quickly, man. My phone is getting wet."

Just when Max had finally wrestled with the canvas side and the slightly damp visitors were snug inside, the rain stopped, just as suddenly as it had started. The clouds parted and the sun continued its barrage on the earth.

During the entire downpour, Abigail had tried to climb under the seats of the Land Rover, now she gave a wail. "Oh, no. My hair will frizz."

A dripping Max smiled thinly at the girl, climbed back into his seat, and headed back in the direction of the lodge, the tires sloshing through the mud. However, the puddles had all dried up by the time they reached the lodge and the sizzling heat had returned.

When Dexter climbed out of the truck, his hand briefly touched the scorching metal side, and he pulled his hand back in shock.

"Careful. You could fry an egg on that," said Max.

CHAPTER 8

That afternoon, the wavy heat returned and the puddles that had been left by the rains earlier that morning shrunk and shrivelled away.

Under a cluster of spiny silver-leaf Terminalia trees, the crash still snoozed, later than usual. A faint hint of silver-green on the tips of the bare branches and a few tiny white flowers, hinted at the hope of more rain. Even so, they provided little shade.

Although she appeared fast asleep, Lindi's radar ears moved constantly, and she picked up the sound of the clattering safari truck as it rumbled down the dusty track.

The bang that followed had her up and snorting, causing the rest of the crash to leap up huffing; prepared to either take flight or fight. Horns facing danger, they formed a protective circle around the stunned youngsters who sat blinking in the middle.

Stepping out in front, Gogo lifted her head and scented the air, ears swivelling listening for sounds. Then she heard it, a low warbling whistle. It triggered a distant memory of when she was young, and an upright human clad in green saved her from those who carried death-spitting sticks. From time to time, she had caught the familiar scent or seen these Uprights from a distance, but they never approached her, always allowing Gogo to come to them if she wanted to. The watcher human would whistle and back slowly away, leaving her in peace.

"I know that sound. It's okay."

Glancing at Gogo, Lindi stepped out in front of Ntombi before she would dash away towards the danger. "No. They are dangerous. It's an Upright."

"No, no. This one is a Watcher-Upright."

Peering around her mother's pillar-like legs, Ntombi strained to get a better look at the object that was causing so much agitation. "What's dat?"

"Just an upright that I see sometimes. They are always watching."

"Just watching?" said Balega. Looking in the direction of the still crouching uprights, he shrugged and started to chomp the dry brown grass at his feet.

"I don't like it," said Lindi.

"I tell you, Lindi. It's okay."

Still, Lindi was not convinced. She knew that Gogo was wise and had kept the crash safe for many years, but her own experiences made her wary of these creatures.

"How do you know it's safe?"

Whilst Lindi and Gogo were heatedly discussing the dangers—or lack of—Ntombi had managed to sneak around her mother and was strutting towards the small huddle of creatures squatting under a thorn tree.

Head held high; she approached them. *Huff, huff, puff, puff,* went Ntombi, leaping back in

127

surprise when the green-coloured watcher huffed back. Whirling around, she raced back to the protection of her mother.

Building up her courage, Ntombi tried again. Showering them all with red-grey dust when she stopped just short of them. "Huff, Puff. Go away!"

One upright had a different sound to the others, a hushed clicking and whirring.

"Go away," she huffed.

Click, click, whirr.

Whirling and twirling, Ntombi danced in front of this clicker, showing off until Lindi suddenly looked away from Gogo and spotted how close she had gotten to the danger.

Rushing over to her daughter, snorting, and kicking dust at the offensive uprights, one of them quickly stood and spun on his two spindly legs to make a hasty getaway. "Ntombi! Get away."

"But Mama...."

Sternly Lindi turned on her daughter and gave her a firm shove, away from the crouched clicking human. "No. Stay here."

Stumbling, Ntombi tried to get around her mother, but Lindi's bulk stood fast and Ntombi finally conceded that her mother meant business. With a little squeak she followed the others as they walked away from the group of humans, heads swaying side to side as they grazed on the grasses at their feet.

Following behind her daughter, Lindi shook her head at Ntombi. "Maiwe, you will be the death of me."

A scream from one of the humans behind them had the Rhinos break into a crashing run, Ntombi cantering in front of her mother as Lindi urged her forward.

Later, after they had returned to the lodge and Max had managed to change out of his wet clothes, they all sat around the table having a light lunch. The ceiling fan overhead whined and squeaked as the rain that had fallen only an hour or so before hadn't had much effect on the sweltering heat. With a contented sigh, Max swallowed the last mouthful of peach cobbler and turned to his unusually quiet guests.

"You guys fancy trying again this evening? Could maybe do a short walk as well as a drive."

"I'm not going out again in the rain," said Theo.

"The rain this morning caught us by surprise, I know, but we could catch the Rhino having a mud wallow."

"No. I'm not going. Too hot anyway. Take the kids, so they won't bother me. Abigail, take a nice photo of a Rhino for Daddy."

With a nod, Max turned towards them. Dexter had gone back for second helpings of the dessert and was greedily attacking it as if there was no tomorrow.

Abigail looked at him in disgust. "How can you eat all that?"

Shrugging, Dexter barely looked up even when Max cleared his throat to get their attention.

"So, we'll venture out then later when it's a little cooler. Remember to cover up, Abi, and Dexter please wear decent shoes. We'll try to take a short walk."

Each gave a grunt in reply, pushed their chairs back with a scrape and left the table, ambling towards the pool.

With a sudden thought, Max called to Dexter, hurrying up to the boy when he was ignored. "Dex, I wondered if you would like to borrow my GoPro. You can film our walk. You can strap it to your hat or your chest or even put it on a selfie stick. Would be great to get footage when we go to the bush camp for canoeing in a few days."

"Sure, why not. Would be great to use on the canoeing, I suppose."

It was as if the rains had not happened, the earth had returned to the dry dustiness and only a few puddles remained. Even those were drying up fast as the sun continued to assault the earth.

The truck screeched to a sudden halt as Max noticed the man in green standing by the side of the track. Shaking the man's hand, African style: a series of pumps and hand over hands later, Max smiled. "Howzit, Twanda. How's the family and the new little Twanda Junior?"

"Hey, Max. All good. Junior is strong like a buffalo, just like his father."

"Excellent. Aren't you supposed to be on leave?"

"Leave's been cancelled, there's been a report of suspected poachers. There are not enough Rangers, so I had to come back."

"Ahh No. I'll keep a lookout too. Seen any Rhino?"

"Ja. Just through the silver-leafed Terminalia trees. They are not going too far from the small puddle of water."

"They not been going to the dam then?"

"Hayi. Too far for the little ones."

The faint whirr of a camera could be heard from Dexter who had, with the speed of his generation, figured out how the GoPro worked and had it filming already.

"Max, what does Hayi mean?"

"It means no in the local language. I think we might take a little stroll, to see if we can get a good view of these Rhino."

Eagerly, they all climbed out of the car, and Dexter slammed the car door with a bang.

"Shhh, you moron," said Abigail.

"Shut up, Princess."

"Right, guys. You do remember the safety talk?"

Both heads nodded eagerly.

Lowering his voice to a staged whisper, Max continued, pleased at how these two had changed towards the wildlife in just a short space of time. "But just to reiterate. We'll walk in a straight line, and when we get closer, we will crouch lower. I will signal with my hand," said Max.

Lowering his hand to indicate what he meant, Max looked at them to ensure that his instructions were clear.

Copying Max's whisper, Dexter raised his hand slightly to ask, "Why do we crouch?"

"It breaks up our form. Humans are the only animals that walk upright; this way we won't be as threatening," replied Twanda.

"Twanda will lead us in. He follows the Rhino all the time and it means that they are a little more habituated to his presence, especially the old Gogo."

"What's a Gogo?" whispered Abi.

"Gogo means grandmother and it's what we have nicknamed the old Matriarch."

"Remember, if they do charge us—don't just run, find a tree if you need to. Twanda, let's go."

Hunched over like old people with a walking stick, they approached the grazing Rhino. As they got closer, the crunching grinding noise of their teeth could be heard as they chomped the dry brittle grass, little squeaks and huffs coming from the little one who peeked out from behind her mother, as they crouched under a small Acacia tree.

Gradually, the calf's curiosity got the better of her and she came over to investigate, huffing and puffing as she approached them. With every photographic click or whirr her ears twitched. Overcoming her fear, she danced in front of them, dust swirling around her feet. Suddenly, the mother decided enough was enough and snorted in the direction of the crouched humans, causing Dexter to get to his feet. The movement was too much for the mother and with another snort, she turned and pushed her baby out in front of her, making her move away to follow the now retreating rumps of the rest of the crash.

Moving to take another step away from the Acacia tree, Dexter let out a screech of pain, as a long thin pointy Acacia thorn pierced the sole of his blue Crocs and embedded itself securely in Dexter's foot.

Both Max and Twanda rushed to Dexter's side, as the Rhino fled in terror from the sound of his blood-curdling shout. Thumping down on his rear end in the dust, Dexter held his foot high in the air, a cluster of white thorns glinting against the blue of the shoe.

"Are you all right, Dex?" said Max.

"Get it out. Get it out!"

With the help of Twanda, Max managed to pry the offensive thorn from its new home, whilst Dexter screamed bloody murder.

Meanwhile, Abigail grinned at her stepbrothers" pain, phone in hand, as she watched his white sports sock turn red. "Smile Dexter."

Leaning on Max, Dexter managed to hop and limp back to the truck and its first aid box.

Placing a bandage over the piercing on the boy's foot, Max patted his knee, then handed him the white thorn, about the length of a finger.

"Here's a trophy for you. Now you know why I told you to put better shoes on."

Taking pity on the boy who sat on the tailgate of the Land Rover whilst being bandaged, Max changed the subject. "What an awesome sighting."

Flicking through the pictures and videos on her phone, Abigail gushed, "That little Rhino was just too cute. I'm sure to get loads of followers now. I even got a few selfies, not to mention Dexter screaming like a baby."

Gritting his teeth, Dexter settled into the back of the Land Rover. "Shut up Abigail."

Climbing into the truck next to Dexter, Abigail caught a whiff of a strong and pungent stench and wrinkled her nose. "What is that awful smell? Dexter put your shoes back on."

"Oh, that's the flower of the silver-leafed Terminalia tree. See? Them, there. They are small white flowers but they let off a terrible smell, especially towards dusk."

The night hummed with Crickets and Mosquitos and the occasional churr of a Nightjar,

136

as Ntombi moved rhythmically through the tall yellowing grasses, grazing. Next to one of Ntombi's huge funnel-like ears, Tubi slept; his head under a wing, swaying with the movements of her head.

Not far away, Lindi tried to graze as well, but no sooner had she put her head down to graze than she'd lift her head again to peer into the black night, ears twitching. She didn't like it here; it was far too close to the Demoni waterhole and its dangers. The rest of the crash were scattered nearby, the yellow grass was still dry and brittle, and most were trying to find the small green shoots at the base of the grass.

The dry air blew gusts of fragrant earth, covering the Lumber-beast in a fine red powder. It was this wind that brought a pungent acrid smell to Lindi's nostrils. She whipped her head up yet again with a snort, startling Sisi who had wandered over.

"What is it, Lindi?"

"What's that smell?"

Raising her head and with a strong snort, Sisi inhaled deeply.

"Something's wrong."

Then they heard the crackling roar and out of the darkness, a red flickering lethal blaze scorching all in its path, the flames licked higher and higher with intense heat. The two mothers frantically looked about for their babies, as Gogo snorted in terror.

"Aiy!" We must go now! Go! Now!"

Spinning on her hindquarters, Gogo fled away from the glowing blaze.

Then things got worse, a lot worse.

Tubi was screaming his warning cry, "Tsk, Tsk, Kirr Kirr."

The rest of the crash galloped after Gogo as the blaze engulfed all in its path. Zebra and Wildebeests crashed through the dry undergrowth in terror, desperate to get away.

Eyes wild, Lindi spun away from the scorching, blazing fire, calling to Ntombi to follow but Ntombi stood transfixed, staring at the thing that flickered in front of her.

"How pretty," said Ntombi, walking towards it. Flames leapt up, making Ntombi jump back; she was so close she could feel its sizzling blistering heat.

"Ntombi!" screamed Lindi, "Get away!"

Using her body, she came between the flickering glow and her baby, the smell of burning flesh filling the air as Lindi screamed in pain and then at her baby— "GO! NOW!"

Pushing her daughter roughly, Lindi turned them away from the red-hot beast to follow the rest of the crash.

But it was too late. The flames leapt higher, surrounding them. Lindi found a gap and they ran to get through the thick smoke before the inferno consumed them both. Just as they thought that they were free, Ntombi heard a strange sound reverberating through the giants.

Rat-a-tat-tat. Blam.

Ntombi squealed in fright as Lindi was flung backwards with force. Then it was chaos.

Tubi was flapping above screaming, the roaring flames flicking and crackling higher and higher towards him. Tubi was forced to fly up to get away from the red-hot roaring fire and the dense dark grey smoke until he was lost from view completely.

"RUN, Ntombi. RUN!"

At the sound of her mother's voice, Ntombi spun around and set off at a gallop with Lindi panting behind her, urging her on.

Rat-a-tat.

Looking over her shoulder at her mother, she saw Lindi's legs crumble, and she crashed to the ground. Spinning round, Ntombi ran to her mother's side.

"Mama!" she screamed, rushing at the Uprights as they surrounded Lindi.

Something hit Ntombi over the head with a solid thud and she fell into an unconscious heap.

CHAPTER 9

Around a table in the dining room, Max sat with Vusa, the lodge manager, discussing the day's sighting.

"It was great to see the new calf, Vusa. But they were so close to the boundary fence."

"They should be okay there, Max."

"If we don't get more rain, they'll drink at that waterhole on the other side, the fence is down."

"Again? It's just been repaired."

"That's Poacher's Corner, for sure. I know the Rangers are doing their best to patrol the fence line, but a shortage of Rangers on the anti-poaching team makes it difficult."

At another table nearby, Abigail and Dexter were huddled around an open laptop arguing over the footage and photos that Abi had posted on social media, especially over the footage of Dexter and the thorns. At the mention of the Rangers and Rhino, both heads shot up.

Theo leaned against the bar, drink in hand. His laptop was open and Abigail's photos of the Rhino on her social media were visible on the screen.

"Daddy, you liked my photos?"

"Hmm. Yes, of course. Great picture, princess. A good horn on that one."

Beaming at her father's interest, she turned to Max. "Why is there a Ranger shortage?"

"Not enough funding," said Max.

"FIRE!"

A loud shout filled the room and a hush followed. The guests—who were enjoying cocktails either at the bar or sipping coffee around the fire pit—panicked. The frenzied sounds of scraping chairs echoed around the room as some of the other visitors got hastily to their feet, looking about them for the nearest exit.

Noticing the look of terror on his young guest's faces, Max turned to the man in green. "Where?"

"In the park. Western boundary."

Turning pale, Max looked over at the Ranger and then back to Vusa. "Oh god, the Rhino. This fire's no accident."

The Ranger nodded rapidly. "We need extra men."

"I'll help where I can," said Max.

"Us too," said Abigail.

The others hadn't noticed that Theo had joined them, their attention fully on the Ranger.

"No. There are men out there with guns. We stay here."

"I agree, Theo. You must stay here in the lodge."

"What if the fire reaches the lodge? I've spent a lot of money on this holiday."

"The lodge staff will look after you."

"But I paid extra for YOU to look after us," said Theo.

"This will be catastrophic for the park and its wildlife. I must help."

With that Max turned on his heel and followed the Ranger towards the parked Land Rovers, leaving his guests staring after him.

The first to recover was Theo, who scoffed in disgust and then returned to his laptop.

"The nerve of the man. Leaving us for some stupid fire."

Joining the rest of the guests around the fire pit, Abigail and Dexter sat in silence as they sipped on a hot chocolate and stared at the amber-red glow of the fire that could just be seen from the lodge nestled in the rocks. A distant rumble of thunder and a brief flash of lightning lit up the horizon and, for a split second, you could make out the ghostly granite balancing boulders.

The first pitter-patter of raindrops made the fire hiss and spit. Everyone ran for cover as the rain fell harder, most deciding that it was time for bed. Dexter and Abigail reluctantly did the same, leaving Theo still hunched over his laptop.

Back in their room, Abigail thumped on her bed. This trip was not turning out how she had expected. She still had not done any riding and her father was still busy working even though they were thousands of miles away from his office. Her phone pinged, indicating that she'd received another message, and then it pinged again and again. Bounding over to Dexter she shoved the phone under his nose, in front of his Nintendo, he tried to flick her away as if she was an annoying Fly.

"Go away."

"Look! I'm famous. Look at all these comments asking for more information about the Rhino. They're even commenting about you and asking how big that thorn was."

"No way. Let me see."

They spent the next few minutes reading the comments, then Dexter had an idea. Walking onto the balcony of their room, he looked out at the glowing fire in the distance. The rain still pattered on the thatched roof, and the clouds covered the Milky Way that could normally be seen stretched far above.

Turning back into the room, Dexter looked at Abigail thoughtfully. "We could be famous. Let's get more footage."

"Is the fire too far away to get any decent shots?"

"Let's find out."

The next morning, Dexter and Abigail were already tucking into a hearty breakfast—well, Dexter was, and Abigail was picking at her fruit platter—when a filthy Max staggered in, his face blackened with soot. Grimly he staggered past them towards the breakfast counter. Wrinkling her nose, Abigail coughed as she got wind of Max; a pungent scent of bush, acrid smoke and sweat seemed to ooze out of his every pore and clung to his weary body.

Pouring himself a huge mug of black coffee, thick like treacle, from the pot on the breakfast table, Max took a seat opposite and slurped at the hot liquid. "Morning, you lot."

"What happened? Did you put out the fire?" Dexter demanded.

"We did. The rain was a godsend."

"What about the Rhinos?" said Abigail.

Rubbing his red-rimmed eyes tiredly, Max looked at them, wondering briefly where all this concern had come from.

"It was a trap. We found the fuel cans that someone had used to start it."

"Someone? Who'd want to start a fire out here?" asked Dexter.

"Poachers."

"What about the Rhino? Our fans will be upset if anything happens to that baby," said Abigail.

Blinking at Abigail, Max wiped a hand over his eyes, leaving a streak down his blackened face.

"Yeah. We've thousands of fans on social media. You must find out what has happened to the Rhino."

"Look, guys, the Rangers are still out there but we are leaving today remember? Going to the bush camp for canoeing."

Putting his coffee mug to his lips, Max drained the last of his coffee and went to get a refill. Hushed whispers came from Abigail and Dexter, their heads together. A frown creased Max's forehead as he thought, what are these two up to? He shrugged, too tired to wonder what had caused the two to suddenly like each other. He was on his way back to the table when Abigail stood up from the table and stamped her foot. The other guests looked up in disgust.

"I don't want to go canoeing. I want to find the Rhino. The fans need to know."

"Shh, Abi. It's all booked," said Max.

"Well, unbook it," said Dexter.

"I'm not sure that's possible, besides your father might want to go. You ask him."

Behind them, Theo appeared, in a crisp blue shirt and chinos. "Ask me what?"

Taking in Max's dishevelled appearance, he sniffed and held his nose in disgust. "Good god, man. You could have washed."

"Daddy. Max has just got back from helping with the fire. He won't let us go looking for the Rhino," said Abigail.

"As I said, we have the canoeing trip booked."

A thin wail came from the girl and her father hastily tried to calm her down.

"It's already booked Princess."

"I WANNA STAY HERE."

"Okay. Okay. Change it, Max?"

With a resigned sigh, Max turned to walk towards the lodge's office.

"I'll see what I can do."

A short while later Max returned, he'd had a quick shower and was looking a lot more like his usual self in his guide's uniform of Khaki shorts and shirt. He grabbed yet another mug of coffee. "Right. I have managed to delay your trip to the bush camp and canoeing until tomorrow, but you'll lose your money if you change it again."

"Happy, Princess? But we leave tomorrow. I won't lose the money I spent on the canoeing." Pleased that he had averted another temper tantrum, Theo sighed in relief.

However, the sly look that passed between Dexter and Abigail was missed by the adults, however, and with a self-satisfied smile on her lips, Abigail looked at Max. "Hurry up! Let's go then."

"Go where? I thought you wanted to stay here?"

"We're going to look for a Rhino."

"That's not a good idea Abi. Why don't you stay here, and I'll go with the Rangers and let you know," said Max.

149

The adults looked at them in shock when both Dexter and Abigail stood up.

"No. We're going, too."

"Will it be dangerous?" asked Theo.

"It could be. If a Rhino is wounded," said Max.

"We'll stay in the truck with you, Max."

Then Abigail changed her tactic and grabbed Max's hands in her own. "Please, please, please. We can film it. Think how good it will be if we find them."

"I suppose that would be okay. But you stay in the truck."

A series of nods all around.

"Okay. Pack your stuff and make sure you bring suitable clothing."

Shaking his head and smiling, Max thought that this was not at all expected. "Are you okay with this, Theo?"

"Sure. It'll keep them out of my hair whilst I finish up a few things."

Then his phone jangled from his top pocket. He walked away as he answered it. "Hello. I don't have it yet. I'm expecting a large deposit any day now. Yes, but—"

"Is that Mum? Can I talk to her?" said Dexter.

Ignoring Dexter, Theo walked rapidly away, and the faint snippets of conversation trailed away. "I'll get my lawyer to call, Sharon, and then it'll—"

Turning, Dexter stomped off towards the vehicle and climbed in, folding his arms across his chest. He was certain that was his mother on the phone. Why wasn't she speaking to him? Since they left on their safari, Dexter hadn't spoken to his mother at all. Something was up, he just knew it.

"Right. Seeing as you've convinced me of this, we'd better get out there. Have you both got sunscreen and water bottles? What about a trip to the loo?"

"Don't need to go now," said Abigail.

"You sure? It might be ages before we get back here."

Stubbornly the girl pouted. Why was Max constantly nagging them about these things?

"No. I'm good."

"What about you Dexter?"

"I'm fine. Let's just go."

At first, it was hard to tell that there had been such drama the night before, all seemed as it should. The Cape Turtle Dove still called out.

"Work harder, work harder."

Clamping his hands over his ears, Dexter tried to block out the persistent bird with a groan. "It doesn't shut up. Blasted thing woke me at four in the morning."

They came round a corner, and everything was charred black; the swaying flaxen grasses reduced to nothing but charred blackened clumps, trees lay where they had crashed still smouldering and the acrid smoke clung to the air. The granite boulders stood among the desolate landscape like tombstones.

"It's so quiet," said Abigail, her hand raised with her phone at the ready to take a selfie, but she couldn't quite bring herself to push the button.

"Yeah," said Dexter. "Even that Dove is now silent."

"And what's that smell?" said Abi.

"Diesel. It's what was used to start the fire."

152

They hadn't gone far when they spotted a Ranger walking along with the road, head down, rifle slung over his shoulder. Slowing the vehicle to a stop, Max called out to the Ranger. "Twanda. Any luck?"

Looking exhausted, the Ranger shook his head, wiping a hand down his face and then down his sooty, muddied olive-green uniform. "Hayi. Nothing. But there's spoor here."

"What's spoor?" said Dexter, switching on the GoPro.

"The footprint or tracks of animals. And people," said Max.

"I'll do another loop and meet you further up the road, Max."

With a nod to Twanda, Max put the vehicle into gear, and they eased slowly forward. "Yebo, Twanda. See you in a bit. Do you guys remember what Rhino spoor looks like?"

"I think so. It has three toes, a larger one at the front and two on either side of it and a wide pad at the back."

"Excellent. Well done. Keep an eye out on the road in front."

The truck crept along the dirt road, all the occupants concentrating on the surroundings looking for signs of life, the thud of the vehicle's engines and the whine of the GoPro the only sounds.

"Wait. Stop!" yelled Abi.

The truck screeched to a halt and Max looked around as if he had missed something. "What is it?"

"I need to pee."

"What? Now?" said Dexter. "Hold it in."

"I can't. I've been holding it in for hours already."

"I told you to go at the lodge," said Max.

"I didn't need to go then."

"Fine. Go behind that tree stump."

"I'm not going outside. What if someone sees me. Take me back to the lodge."

Climbing out of the driver's seat, Max went to the back of the truck, and returned carrying a shovel and a roll of toilet paper. "Abi, I thought you wanted to find the Rhino. If we go back, it'll waste time. You'll have to go here or hold it in."

"What's the shovel for?"

"To bury it."

The look on Abi's face made Dexter burst out laughing, until she turned on him with a look that would have made a snarling Lion slink away with his tail between his legs.

Holding out the shovel and paper, Max grinned. It always amazed him why people struggled with an outside toilet stop. "Look, there's Twanda. I'm sure he'll stand guard whilst you go."

"Fine! Dexter, put that blasted camera away. My fans don't need to see this."

Turning his back, Twanda stood guard, like a sentry outside a palace, a grin on his face.

There was a shout from Abigail, her previous embarrassment forgotten as she came running out from behind the blackened tree trunk. "Hey! I've found something."

Grabbing Max by the arm, she pulled him around the tree, pointing at the brass objects scattered at the base of the trunk.

"That's an AK-47 bullet casing," said Max. Bending down, he picked a handful of the spent casing and dropped them again suddenly as if he'd been bitten. "Ouch, they're still hot from the fire."

"How did they get here?" said Dexter.

"Poachers," replied Max and Twanda together.

Twanda wandered over to where Abigail had found the bullet casings, then moved away, working in a circle, around and around.

"What's he doing?" said Abigail.

"Looking to see if there are any tracks of the Rhino or the poachers."

Eyes wide at a sudden thought, Dexter glanced over his shoulder, half expecting dangerous-looking men to leap out of the bushes at any moment.

"Are they still here?"

Rushing to reassure the boy, Max shook his head. "Probably not. They tend to operate at night. Let's hope that they didn't get what they came for."

They sat in silence, as they waited for the Ranger to return with any news. Around them, small flames still flickered amongst the already charred landscape and fallen trees, smoking and smouldering.

Breaking the stillness, Dexter checked his

watch and tapped Max on the shoulder. "He's been gone a long time."

"He has. It's possible he found some tracks and has his head down following them."

Next to Dexter, Abigail had been filming a short clip on her phone. "It's so sad that this was where we were yesterday, watching that baby Rhino."

"It is. Let's hope that she's okay and that they had gone before the fire started." Max said, wondering how these could possibly be the same two teenagers that arrived only a week ago?

"Max, could this fire affect other things in the Safari Park?" said Dexter.

"Unfortunately, everything that lives here will be affected by this fire in some way. Why don't we climb that boulder and have the lunch that the lodge packed us?"

The three of them scrambled up the scorched boulder. It wasn't the largest of the parks balancing rocks and it took only a few minutes to scale to the top. But it got them out of the smoke a little and gave them a view of the immediate area.

Opening the containers with the lunch they sat again in silence.

"It's so quiet and still," whispered Abigail.

"Yeah, even that Turtle Dove has shut up," said Dexter.

Swallowing a mouthful of a cheese sandwich, Max nodded at his young guests. "It's unnatural, hey?"

"Look! The Ranger," said Dexter, pointing at the ground below.

Sure enough, the Ranger was trotting towards them, and it didn't take him long to join them on their rock.

Wordlessly, Max passed him the sandwich box and a bottle of water, waiting for the man to take a swig. Downing the water in one go, Twanda, the Ranger, handed the empty bottle back to Max. "I found blood spoor and Rhino tracks but still no sign of them. But there are Zebra and Wildebeest tracks over the top of the Rhino."

Rubbing his eyes, Max shook his head. "Aiy. That's not good, Twanda. We'll drive to see if we can pick up anything."

With a sharp nod, the Ranger got up, finished his sandwich, and bound off the rock. With a brief wave, he walked off in the direction he had come, his footsteps flicking up the ash of what remained of the bush.

Max and the youngsters drove around for several hours after lunch, until their eyes stung from the smoke and their throats felt as parched as the landscape around them.

Eventually, Max stopped the truck to turn to the teens. "It's getting late, guys. Time head back."

Both Abigail and Dexter nodded, distraught that there was still no sign of the Rhino or the Game Ranger.

With a final look about her, Abigail wiped sweaty soot from her face. "Max, what about the Ranger?"

"He'll continue looking and make his own way back."

Back at the lodge the children eagerly dived into the pool, still dressed in their safari clothes. Streaks of black floaty ash followed them, as the water washed off the grime of the day.

On a stool in the corner of the bar, Theo sat with his laptop open. It hadn't taken Theo long to figure that the strongest WIFI was in the bar as it was the closest area to the office. In his opinion, it was a win-win.

He'd barely looked up when Max walked in and motioned to the bartender. "My usual, Shamwari. Siyabonga. You have a good day, Theo?"

"Blasted woman is after more money. Should have been more careful. She's just a—"

Noticing Dexter and Abigail standing just behind Max, towels around their shoulders and dripping water onto the floor, Theodore's menacing words trailed ott.

Clearing his throat Theo smiled brightly. "You two have a good day?"

Without a word, Dexter spun on his heel and left. Shaking her head sadly without saying a word Abigail turned and followed her stepbrother.

It was a very subdued dinner, each thinking about the day. Even Dexter's Nintendo was silent for once, although a faint glow came from Theodore's mobile phone as he stared at it intently.

It was whilst Max, Abigail and Dexter sat around the firepit staring into the flames of what Max called his "bush TV" when a waiter came over to Max and whispered in his ear.

Standing quickly, Max's chair fell to the ground with a thud. "Excuse me."

Turning on his heel, he walked into the lodge. Through the large glass doors, Abi could see him talking with a Ranger. Max gave a nod and walked back over to the firepit; his face grim in the flickering light.

"Would you mind if we leave for the bush camp a little later tomorrow?"

"Why?" Abi wanted to know.

"What's happened?" said Dexter.

"The Rangers need help tomorrow with the Rhino search. Hyena have been heard and they need to check it out."

"We don't mind. Do we, Dexter?" Abigail poked her stepbrother.

Giving a nod, Dexter confirmed his agreement. He wasn't that keen on canoeing anyway, and he'd been told that there was no WIFI.

"I suppose we could film some more."

"No. I think—"

"What's going on?" Theodore interrupted, coming up behind Max from the bar, where he'd been on his laptop since dinner.

"Is it okay if we leave after lunch for the bush camp tomorrow?"

"I thought that's when we were leaving anyway."

"We normally leave after breakfast as it's a long drive."

"As long as we don't miss the canoeing. I will not lose any more money. Get it."

"I'll speak with the lodge, Theo, and ensure that you don't lose your money."

"Daddy," said Abigail. "Can we go with Max tomorrow?"

"Sure. Do what you want."

"I'm not sure that's a good idea," said Max, "It means an early start. Wouldn't you prefer to sleep in?"

"We wanna film it and post it. My fans will love it."

After several minutes of trying to persuade Abigail and Dexter that they should stay, Max gave up. "Fine, but you must be ready before sunup. We leave straight away. Every minute is vital."

CHAPTER 10

The pounding in her head was the first thing that Ntombi became aware of as she slowly woke from what felt like an endless, dreamless sleep. Rubbing the side of her head on her knees, she wondered why her head hurt so much. Gingerly, she tried to shake her head a little to clear the fogginess in her brain, and fought back a wave of nausea, as a sickly-sweet smell filled her nostrils. Placing her two round front feet in front of her, Ntombi stood up, swaying.

Taking a tentative step, she skidded on the dark crimson mud under her, the sweltering heat already humming.

Blinking against the blinding brightness, Ntombi looked around. Where was she? Why was it so quiet? She swiveled her ears trying to catch the slightest sound. No whiny Cicadas, no chirping Tubi. Then from behind her came a faint groan and Ntombi rushed to Lindi, who lay crumpled in the mud, a pool of thick red pungent blood around her head.

Lindi struggled to get up, her feet flailing as she tried to roll over but, in the end, it was too much, and her head flopped back down with a squelch.

Rubbing against her mother, Ntombi shivered, squeaking softly and nudging Lindi's side. "Mama? I'm hungry."

Emitting another faint groan, Lindi's voice was so faint that Ntombi had to strain her trumpet-ears to hear her.

"Ntombi. You—must—go."

"I can't leave you, Mama."

"Find—Gogo."

Rubbing her head against Lindi's, frothy blood smeared across Ntombi's face as Lindi groaned again.

"Get up, Mama. We'll find her together."

Closing her eyes, Lindi did not respond and, despite Ntombi nudging her again and again, she didn't move or speak again. So Ntombi lay down next to her mother, waiting for her to wake from her nap.

A shadow flew across the plains and Ntombi watched the shadow as it fluttered across the blackened landscape. Scrambling to her feet she tried to call out but all too quickly the shadow disappeared, as quickly as it had come.

It continued to warm up, and still the pair lay in the open, exposed to the harsh rays of the sun. Ntombi knew that they should be looking for the cool comfort of shady trees, but Lindi lay still and unresponsive. More shadows fell over Ntombi, as a few large repulsively ugly looking birds flapped gormlessly onto the ground nearby, hissing and squawking.

The Vultures had arrived.

When Ntombi ran at them, they leapt back in shock with their huge wings flapping, their scrawny scruffy necks almost snake-like, unused to their food moving, let alone having a heartbeat. They retreated to a safe distance, their beady dark eyes watching and waiting, like the undertakers of the animal world. Shuddering against her mother's raspy body, Ntombi could smell the Vulture's revolting, stale stench as more joined the others in the carcass of a burnt-out tree, waiting and watching.

A trembling Ntombi lay next to her mother, calling and calling to her lifeless body. When she could muster the energy, she chased the sinister but patient Vultures that waited nearby, hopping closer and closer on their long taloned claws as their strong beaks pecked at her feet. The dusty brown scruffy Vultures would just fly or hop a short distance away and continue their waiting.

Yelling and huffing, Ntombi charged at the Vultures. "What are you waiting for? Go away!"

Then she would turn back to her mother's side, nudge her for milk and when she got no response Ntombi would flop next to her mother, crying out for her.

"Mama. Mama. Mama."

Ntombi's mournful cries carried in the warm twirling wind as the mud dried, the ash from the fire mixed with dust, coating everything, giving the whole area a ghostly appearance.

Wandering what had happed to Sisi, Balega and the crash of Rhino, Ntombi gave a sudden shout. Perhaps they were not far and would help.

"Balega, Gogo, Sisi."

Nothing.

"TUBI."

There was no cheerful chirp from the little dusky brown bird, just the hiss of the waiting Vultures.

The darkness had returned, and still Lindi had not moved. Ntombi kept crying to her mother and nudging her, in the hopes that her mother would roll over and allow her to suckle. At least the skulking Vultures seemed to have given up for the moment, although they had not gone far and were now roosting in the skeletal remains of a tree, their sinister forms silhouetted against the starry sky, as the Milky Way stretched across the sky.

"Mama. Please. Wake up."

The lingering smell of smouldering vegetation mingled with the dried pungent blood, and the faint scent of the death-uprights and their death spitting sticks filled Ntombi nostrils. Looming shadows crept towards the terrified little Rhino, and she shrunk back against her mother, feeling her mother's still body behind her. Swivelling her ears, the sounds of the night filled the air; the trilling Nightjar and chirping Crickets, and a new and terrifying cry that chilled the blood in Ntombi's veins. It started in the distance and seemed to echo through the rocky granite graveyard. Ears down, Ntombi shrunk back and squeaked shakily to Lindi. The low whooping call was followed by a high-pitched giggle.

"Whoop, whoop, whoop-ooo!"

"Mama? Mpisi are coming."

Trying to peer into the gloomy shadows, Ntombi sniffed the air. She was sure something was lurking in the darkness.

Blurry shapes moved through the desolate bush; a glint in the darkness, as a dog-like head appeared and lopped towards them with murderous intent, sharp canine teeth bared. It sniffed deeply, and scenting the blood that covered Lindi, it gave a chilling giggle. The cries of the rest of its clan suddenly seemed to change—from a low whoop to high-pitched giggles—and in the darkness, Ntombi could hear the tearing and crunching as the Hyena found their dinner, a hapless Wildebeest who'd succumbed to the fire. The beast that sniffed at her feet turned and ran back to his laughing clan members.

Trembling against her mother, a warm dusty breeze carried the fetid scent of the whooping giggling creatures of the dark. She lay against Lindi, through the longest, darkest of nights, trying to block out their terrifying sounds.

Crunching bones and squealing giggles continued all through the night and Ntombi lay by Lindi's side, wondering when they would come for them.

Eventually, the first sounds of "work-harder" filled the air. The Cape Turtle Dove was awake, signalling that morning was upon them.

Gratefully, Ntombi closed her eyes, knowing that she would have to get her mother to move from this spot, far away from the scavenging beasts.

The stars still twinkled high above when Max and the youngsters left the lodge the next morning—even the Cape Turtle Doves still slept.

Half-asleep, Abigail swayed in the back of the truck as it trundled down the track. The puddles had all but dried up now and the dust had returned.

Driving quicker than he normally would, Max took them to the spot where they had stopped looking the day before. The calling Dove was now fully awake as the trio drove into the blackened fire-stricken area, the smell of smoke still clung to the air and the odd tree stump still smouldered.

Suddenly, Abigail gave an excited shout causing Max to slam his foot down sharply on the brakes. "What is it, Abi?"

"I'm not sure. But, shh—Listen."

A crunching sound came from the shadows behind a fallen tree, followed by a hysterical giggle, Abigail and Dexter shivered at the chilling sound.

With a sigh, Max turned to them. "Hyena. Let's hope Rhino is not on the menu."

"Cool," said Dexter, "we haven't seen a Hyena yet."

Scrabbling with the GoPro, Dexter made to get out of the truck, but Max stopped him, grabbing his rifle and jumping out.

"Stay here. I'll check it out."

Eyes wide, they sat huddled together, waiting for Max's return, the GoPro clutched firmly in Dexter's hand, Abigail clutching his free hand tightly. What if Max doesn't come back? Moving to switch the GoPro on, Dexter realized that he was holding hands with Abi. He hastily retrieved his hand scoffing, "You scared, Abi? Just like a girl."

"I'm not scared. I thought you were."

A loud shout from Max, had them leaping in their seats, interrupting their bickering.

"Haa. Haa."

All hell broke loose as the burnt bush exploded with half a dozen or so spotted Hyena, fleeing from Max's shouts of anger.

Then Max appeared, carrying his rifle casually in his hand, chuckling as he saw the worried youngsters in the back of the truck.

"Stupid Mpisi," he said, "They were feeding on a Wildebeest."

"What's a Mpisi?" said Dexter.

"Mpisi is the local word for Hyena."

Reaching under the console of the vehicle, Max flicked the two-way radio on. It crackled to life, startling Dexter who squealed. "Hey! When did you fit that? It's so retro."

"It's always been there but I switch it off when we are game driving. Best used for emergencies. Got to notify the Rangers we've found Hyena feeding on a Wildebeest carcass."

"Why don't you just use a mobile phone like normal people?" scoffed Abigail.

"No phone signal, Abi."

The short conversation with the Ranger's base, over the radio, told them that Rangers were still searching and so far, there had been no sightings of the Rhino. Glancing briefly at his watch, Max switched the radio off and turned the vehicle's ignition. "Let's crack on, shall we?"

They hadn't gone far when a Ranger, ran out at them his arms waving wildly, Max slammed on the brakes as he reached them, dust and ash billowing around in great clouds.

"Twanda?"

His chest heaving and dripping with sweat, as if he had just run a double marathon, Twanda struggled to catch his breath, taking a deep shaky breath.

"Bhejane. I—have—found—them."

"Ngaphi? Where?"

"Katshana."

In the back of the truck, Abigail and Dexter felt like they were watching a tennis match, as they struggled to keep up with the animated conversation in the strange-sounding local language. For a moment, Abigail tried to recall what the language was called; Ndebele or Zulu she was sure Max had told them.

"Eh-Eh," said Twanda.

"Right get in, we'll go back to base."

In shock, the young teenagers looked at Max as the engine coughed to life and Max placed his hand on the gearstick. Tapping Max sharply on the shoulder, Abigail almost shouted in his ear.

"Wait. What the—?"

With a side-ways glance at Dexter who'd been filming the whole exchange, Abigail stopped herself, took a breath and finished.

"What's happening?"

"Oh Gosh! Abigail, Dexter! I'd almost forgotten you were here. Twanda has found the Rhino but they're in a bad way," said Max.

"Yebo. Very far from here. I've been running for a long time," said Twanda.

"It is in an area with no roads and is several hours away to walk. We'll head back to get the chopper and a vet."

Clinging to the metal roll bars of the Land Rover, the kids tried to stay in their seats as they sped through the Dwala Safari Park towards the makeshift helipad and the Ranger base.

In the front seat next to Max, Twanda had one hand on the rail in front of him and the other held the radio. "Okay. The vet will meet us at the chopper."

Giving a brief nod, Max kept his eyes on the track, intent on getting them there as quickly and safely as possible. Screeching to a halt near the helipad and the waiting helicopter, they all bailed out and ran towards it.

Leaning against the side of the red chopper was a man dressed in Khaki green, a large black duffel bag with a blue cross on its side at his feet.

Shaking the man's hand, Max turned to the teenagers. "Guys, meet Doctor Ben Moyo."

Stepping forward, Dexter and Abigail went to greet the vet, but he ignored them. He turned, opened the chopper's door, placed his bag inside and climbed in. With a shrug, Max completed his safety inspection and the rest of them clambered aboard the helicopter.

The vet sat tapping his foot on the metal floor, the slight tapping reverberating in the close confines of the hot interior. "What are you thinking, Max. Bringing kids?"

Leaning forward, Max flicked the switch to start the helicopter's rotors and it whirred to life.

"Technically, their father's paying for this, and I believe they're 12 and 13, around the same age as my son, Andy, and he joins us all the time."

Crammed in the back between Abigail and the domed glass door of the chopper, Dexter heard the conversation between the two men in the front and felt a brief hint of jealousy at the thought of Max's son and their relationship. How awesome it must be to spend time with your father doing things like this together. Dexter hadn't seen his father in years, and Theodore was hardly around either.

From above, they could make out the extent of the fire, the blackened area reaching into the healthier plains like fingers. The shadow of the helicopter floated across the landscape below them, like a giant bird. With his head resting on the glass, Dexter watched as the scenery flashed below them, when he spotted a large tan, brown bird, soaring effortlessly beneath them. No sooner had he noticed the first bird than it was joined by another, and another, each of them spiralling round and round in the warm current of air.

Suddenly, one of the birds tucked in its wings and dropped like an arrow towards the blackened earth.

"LOOK!" shouted Dexter. "What's that?"

"Vultures. There. That's what they're after," said Doctor Ben.

Sure enough, they could just make out two dark grey lifeless shapes below. Max banked the chopper sharply, dropping in height to give them a better view.

"It's the Rhino," said Twanda from the back.

"Take us down, Max. Let's hope that we're not too late," said the vet, grabbing his bag.

Max quickly found a suitable flat open area in which to land, the chopper's blades swirling the dust and ash like a mini hurricane. The vet and Twanda had already leapt from the helicopter and were moving rapidly towards the prone Rhino shapes.

The chopper's blades had just stopped spinning when Max turned to the teenagers. "You two stay in the chopper."

"But we wanna film," whined Abigail.

"Stay here. Do I make myself clear?"

"But—" said Dexter, fiddling with the GoPro and attaching it to the strap on his chest.

"But—" With the flick of her hair, Abi retorted, "Daddy said you're supposed to do whatever we want."

"No, I don't. I must keep you safe."

"Spoilt, aren't they?" said Ben, gesturing towards the kids with his thumb.

"They are," agreed Max. "But all they need is their father's attention."

Folding her arms over her chest, Abi thumped back in her seat and started flicking through the apps on her phone. She chucked it down in frustration when she realised there was no signal. "It's not fair. I don't wanna stay in the chopper."

A low mournful squeak mixed with a harsh grating hiss, carried towards them on the wind.

"What's that noise?"

A shiver ran down Dexter's spine, he looked at the hunched bird sitting in the charred tree. "Vultures. They give me the shivers."

"Don't be silly, Dexter. It's just a big ugly bird."

"I know. But they follow death."

"Let's look. We could make it like a documentary."

"I'm not sure, Abi. Max told us to stay here. It could be dangerous."

But Abigail wasn't listening. She was already out of the chopper and striding towards the tree. She called over her shoulder, "Come on. Live a little. Max takes his son, so how dangerous could it be?"

With a sigh, Dexter clambered out of the helicopter and followed his stepsister. They walked slowly in single file as they had been told to do, on what seemed countless walks with Max and other guides on their travels. Dexter had his camera out and was already filming, as Abi motioned to her viewers. They rounded a granite boulder that looked naked without its usual cover of shrubs or greenery. There on the other side lay a female Rhino, crumpled in a heap. Where her horn should have been was a large gaping hole, oozing blood.

The Vultures sat in a twisted burnt skeleton of a tree, the undertakers.

"There's something on the other side of her," said Abigail, walking around.

They could just make out Max and Dr Ben crouched over as they approached the downed Rhino. A grey blur whizzed toward Abi, huffing and puffing, intent on protecting its mother.

Head down, Ntombi meant business and she charged at the pale upright who she was certain had come to harm her. Huffing, she homed in on her target, dark coal-like dust flying from her feet.

In the blink of an eye, Max had sprinted to Abigail and wrenched her out of the way, just in time. The wind from the charging animal gushed past Max and Abigail as Ntombi ran crashed through the burnt Acacia shrubs, the sharp white thorns standing out against their blackened branches.

"Stop!" yelled Ben, "It's wounded."

It was too late, and the little Rhino did not stop or look back.

"Abigail, are you okay?"

"Sorry, Max."

Dusting the dirt and soot from her khaki shorts, Abigail glanced up at Max's face. He was furious. He opened his mouth but before he could say anything, a red-faced Dr Ben stomped over and wagged a finger at her.

"You spoilt brats. Look what you have done. We've lost the calf. If it dies it will be your fault."

Staring at the vet in shock, Abigail opened her mouth. How dare he? The words died on her lips as a startled cry from behind them drew their attention.

They turned to see Twanda, the Game Ranger, kneeling in congealing blood at the head of the Rhino, tears in his dark eyes.

"The female! I think she's breathing."

Ntombi: A Rhino's Story

CHAPTER 11

On and on ran Ntombi, her oval feet thumping on the blackened earth to the same beat as her heart. Exhausted, she collapsed under a scraggly tree and looked around. Everything seemed strange. Where was she? Where was the granite rock Hook-snout? Normally, Hook-snout terrified her but now she longed to find its familiar shape.

In the distance she could just make out another granite giant. It, too, rose from the ochre tree line, like a king on his throne. Gone was the blackened earth; the trees all had a healthy green tinge to them, and at her feet Ntombi felt the gentle tickle of golden grasses. Ntombi gasped for breath, her throat dry and raspy from the dust and smoke that had filled her lungs during the night. Guilt flooded through her—she'd left her mother— but those uprights had terrified her, and she just knew that she had to run. But now she was all alone, and she had no idea what she was going to do. A tear trickled down her cheek. Was there anyone out there?

"Mama? Gogo? Tubi?"

Flopping her head onto the ground in front of her, she closed her eyes, wishing that death would claim her and that this torment would end. She lay where she had collapsed, too exhausted to move and no longer caring what happened to her.

In her fitful dreams, the scary upright humans rushed at her pulling at her, tugging at her ears. She heard her mother's voice calling, telling her to run, run and find Gogo. The tugging grew stronger, and the stench of death filled her nostrils and she puffed and panted trying to flee her nightmare.

"Leave me alone!"

Pain coursed through her head as the tugging grew more violent and a ripping sound filled her head, as the top of her ear gave way. The pain was so intense that she woke with a jolt and turned to face her attacker with a shout. "OWWW!"

Blinking hard, blood oozed from the remains of her ear, droplets of crimson red flicked over the dry dusty earth and yellowing grass.

There in front of her was the furry head of a spotted Hyena, with rounded ears and sharp canine teeth, titbits of her ear dangling from its grinning jaws. Spinning around, Ntombi fled, the cackling thing in hot pursuit snapping at her tail. Then just when Ntombi felt she could run no longer, a small brown blur streaked passed and flew at her pursuer, squawking and chattering, beating its wings. The Hyena leapt back in shock; how could such a small insignificant bird have the audacity to attack him.

Bravely the little brown Oxpecker flew again and again at the Hyena shouting and flapping his wings and tapping it sharply on the snout. Once. Twice. Peck. Peck. "Back! Back!"

The Hyena howled—no meal was worth this abuse—it tucked its short tail between its legs and with high pitched squeal scurried away.

With a satisfied huff, Tubi yelled after the Hyena's retreating sloping back. "And don't come back!"

Cowering under a bush Ntombi shivered at the sounds behind her and turned when she heard Tubi call softly to her.

"Tubi? Is that you?" Rubbing what was left of her ear on the ground to relieve the stinging pain, Ntombi turned to her plucky little feathered friend. "You saved me."

Landing on Ntombi between her eyes and above her stubby horn, Tubi laid his head on her. "Are you okay?"

Ntombi nodded, still trembling with shock. The stinging from her ear made her eyes weep. "Has it gone?"

"For now, but we must leave this place, Ntombi. It will come back in the dark."

Long shadows were already casting across the plains, making Ntombi aware of the impending night. She knew Tubi was right; they couldn't stay here but she had no idea where to go or what to do.

"Where is Lindi?" asked Tubi.

"Death-Uprights got us. Is Mama with you?"

"Aiy, Ntombi. No Lindi."

"What about Gogo and the crash?"

"Aiy, nobody. Just you."

With a sob Ntombi flopped her head onto her knees, crying for her mother. She wanted her mother's warm comforting body. "It's my fault. Mama told me I would be the death of her. I was too naughty. It's my fault."

Patting her on her head with his wing, Tubi tried to comfort his friend, but he was anxious to get her away from this place. The Hyena would come back and bring the rest of his clan. "Come, let's find a safe place to rest."

They trudged through the dusty earth of the Safari Park. Shadows lengthened and the sky blushed red as the sun dipped below the horizon. All too soon it was dark. For the traumatized pair danger seemed to stare out from everywhere and with each sound, Ntombi would flinch, certain that Hyena or the humans were going to finish her.

They came to an outcrop of rocky giants. Backing against the hard rough granite surface Ntombi sank thankfully to the ground, placing her large square snout in front of her.

"When we've rested, we'll find Gogo," said Tubi.

Ntombi wearily closed her eyes, but sleep would not come. Every sound terrified her, and she kept jumping up with a snort, scenting the air every few minutes in case of danger or the Death-Uprights returning. Eventually, exhaustion took over and Ntombi drifted into a fitful sleep.

She dreamed of terrifying wingless flappers that made such awful sounds and bought such strong winds—whop, whop, whop—and the cackling whooping cry of Mpisi the Hyena mingled together with the terrified cries of her mother.

Poor Tubi did not fare much better; it had been terrifying when the blazing fire had torn through the plains, its ravenous appetite consuming all in its path. Flames had licked through the trees, and dense black billowing smoke made it hard for him to find his host and friend, Ntombi. The Rhino crash and many of the other animals had fled in terror and the bad uprights humans had come. Tubi had not seen what happened to Lindi or Ntombi. In the end, he had followed a herd of Zebra and found safety away from the fire. When Tubi awoke the next morning, the Zebra herd had gone and he knew that he had to find Ntombi, Gogo and the rest of the Rhino crash. He had spent the next few days searching; he was lucky to have found Ntombi when he did. But what if he couldn't find Gogo? Without his flock, he was just one tiny bird and he dearly felt he needed the many eyes that his flock provided. Perhaps, he thought, I could find other friends to help us.

With that lingering thought, he fell into a troubled sleep.

It seemed like she had hardly slept at all when Tubi jumped onto Ntombi's head and pecked at her good ear.

"Up and at them, girly. Time to find Gogo."

Ntombi clambered wearily to her feet, yawning widely, with the impatient Tubi flapping and chirping to get her going.

"Let's go. It's not safe here, we need to find Gogo."

"Which way, Tubi? Mama always knew the way."

Twitching to get going the little bird flapped into the air, getting as high as he could, chirping as he flew. "I'll check it out."

Had it only been two days since they had last seen the Rhino all happy, safe, and enjoying a nap in the midday sun? To Abigail and Dexter, it seemed like a lifetime ago when they sat back at the lodge, their luggage packed for their canoeing trip, waiting for Max who was trying to get news of the baby Rhino and her mother. The earlier shout from Twanda the Ranger had everyone rush to the aid of the mother; the little calf forgotten. The mother Rhino lay coated in her blood, most of her face viciously hacked, broken bits of bone visible, every so often she would gasp, sucking air through her smashed nasal passage choked with blood, bone, and desiccated flesh.

Turning away from the sight, tears streaming down their faces, Abigail and Dexter clasped each other's hands as they tried to overcome their emotions.

Springing into action, the Vet dug in his bag, administered both painkillers and an antibiotic, he looked up briefly from his work to bark, "Get those brats out of here. They'll just get in the way."

Max had been so engrossed in helping Dr Ben and the Rhino that he had completely forgotten his young charges, who stood huddled together with their backs against the charred remains of a tree. One look at their faces told him that the vet was right, this was no place for the youngsters.

Just as Max reached them, Dexter turned away from Abigail and threw up the contents of his stomach onto the blackened ground.

"Come on, guys. Let's head back to the lodge. Let the vet do his job."

When they had gotten back to the lodge, Max sat the shocked teenagers in the comfy lounge chairs and made them each a cup of sweet tea, with so many heaped teaspoons of sugar that the spoon almost stood up on its own. Both Abigail and Dexter drank their tea without any complaints, their faces white, as their shaking hands clasped their mugs. There had been no sign of the little Rhino after she had charged Abigail. Everyone feared the worst; it wasn't safe for a young Rhino to be out there deprived of its mother. Certainly, that's what Max had told them; a Rhino mother can protect its young from most predators but a baby on its own could easily fall prey to Hyenas or Lions.

The pair looked up eagerly when Max walked in but one look at his face told them that he didn't have good news.

"Nothing, I'm afraid."

He wiped his hand across his bloodshot eyes, stubble sprouting on his normally well-shaved chin, his clothes streaked with soot and blood. Max noticed that Abigail and Dexter looked as dishevelled as he did. Abigail who was normally so well turned out had dust, ash, blood, and a few splatters of vomit on her; she was obviously too close to Dexter when he threw up. Dexter didn't look much better, he still looked like he could spew again at any given moment. "Why don't we all have a shower. It will make us feel so much better. Then we'll make our way to the bush camp."

"But what about the Rhino?" Abigail asked.

"I think we should leave the Rangers and the veterinary team to do their jobs."

They were too exhausted to argue and nodded; they shakily got to their feet and walked off towards their room.

A little later, Max walked into the thatched main building of the lodge and found Abigail and Dexter both looking refreshed, colour back on their faces. In the corner of the lounge, Theodore sat frowning into his phone. They looked up when Max walked in.

"Look here. What's the idea of upsetting the children like that?" said Theodore.

Opening his mouth, Max started to apologise but was interrupted when Dexter indicated that Max should join them.

"Come see. We've been looking at our footage."

A laptop sat open on the table in front of the pair, the footage flicking across the screen.

Theodore stood up briskly and pushed his phone into his top pocket. "Good footage. Let's go now. Time is money."

Ignoring her father, Abigail tried to push the laptop towards Max.

"And look at all the likes and comments we've had on social media. Everyone is hoping that we find that baby soon."

Turning to head toward his room a thought struck Max, he turned back to them. "Guys, did you use a phone for any of these images?"

"Uh-huh," said Abigail.

"There's a slim chance that the poachers may have used the geotag on the photo to locate the Rhino. Remember I talked about this during my safety talk when you guys first got here," Max continued.

Shrugging, Abigail looked at the images that flashed on the FlikFlak and the video of herself looking grimly into the camera as she explained the scene behind her. "What's that? Sounds nerdy."

"Don't you know anything, Abigail? A Geotag is an electronic tag that assigns a geographical location to a photo or video," scoffed Dexter.

"Oh yeah. I remember. I'm sure I switched it off."

Nodding, Max turned and walked off towards his room.

When Max returned, Theodore was pacing up and down in front of the lodge entrance, constantly looking at his gold watch. He looked up with a loud sigh. "About time. Took you long enough. Now let's go and get this canoeing over with."

"Right. Okay then. The Landy's ready."

"No. No. I want the chopper. Be quicker."

"But it's a lovely drive through the park and then along the river."

"No. I'm paying for this, and I want the chopper."

Sighing and mentally cursing himself for accepting this safari, when he could be out on patrol helping the anti-poaching unit or looking for the baby Rhino, Max nodded. "Fine. You're the boss. The truck can take us to the helipad then. Come on, you two."

Behind Max, Dexter and Abigail jostled each other, the sounds of their whispered bickering, barely audible.

"You do it."

"No. You're his princess. You do it."

Taking a deep breath, Abigail turned to her father who now stood with his hands on his hips. She fluttered her eyelashes and her voice turned sickly sweet, "Daddy. Can't we stay and help them look for the Rhino. Please."

Her father was already shaking his head, but Max beat him to it.

"Not a good idea. Dr Ben is still annoyed with you two."

"He's a horrid rude man," said Abigail.

"Ben's skill as a vet is second to none, but his people skills not so much. The Rangers will let us know any news."

When they reached the makeshift helipad, Theodore waited until the children were strapped in the back and Max was walking around the chopper doing his usual safety checks.

"I have urgent business I need to attend to. Once we are done with the canoeing, I want you to drop me at the airport and then bring the kids back here. I'll only be gone a few days."

Banging his head on the belly of the chopper, Max cursed and rubbed the back of his head as he turned to face Theodore. "You can't leave me with the kids. I'm not a babysitter. It's one thing to stay in the camp when I take them on activity but to leave me with them for a few days. Out of the question."

"I'll make it worth your while."

"But—"

Then Max thought of the good he could do for the Rhino, sighed, and nodded in agreement.

"Fine. But you must tell them yourself."

Ntombi: A Rhino's Story

CHAPTER 12

The rain had left behind small puddles but not enough to drink from, and with the rising heat they were drying up fast, leaving behind a dry cracked patch of dirt. Still, the little bit of rain had given new life to the dead dry vegetation and was starting to show signs of rebirth. Bright green shoots grew along the track and the shade-givers sported tiny buds too.

Flitting from tree to tree, Tubi kept a worried eye on his friend. She trudged along behind him, her head low, dust trailing behind her.

Jumping at every little sound, Ntombi followed her feathered friend, and Tubi had a job keeping her calm, especially during the dark long nights. He knew that they needed to find Gogo, the Rhino's matriarch, quickly if they were to survive.

"Howzit, guys?"

A nearby voice made them jump. Ntombi snorted in fear and Tubi leapt into the air, calling his warning cry.

"Steady on, it's me."

"Oh, Jabu! It's you!" breathed Ntombi.

Sitting down with a thump as her shaking legs gave way, Ntombi tried to slow her thumping heart as she stared at the bedraggled, scruffy Baboon.

Looking at her two friends, Jabu could see that something was wrong. Ntombi was hunched and shaking, and Tubi seemed to have lost his chirp, his normal bright red and yellow beak seemed to lack its usual lustre.

"What's wrong? Where's Lindi?"

"A bad thing has happened. Mama was hurt by Death-Uprights, and we've lost her. We have to find Gogo."

A single tear rolled down Ntombi's cheek.

"Aiy, it is bad, very bad."

Jabu was looking scruffier than usual. Her shaggy fur was matted and dirty and her curvy tail was crusted with weeping swollen sores, Flies swarming over it like Vultures on a kill.

"Jabu, what happened to you?" asked Tubi.

Shaking her head, Jabu recounted the story of when the fire came and of how the flames roared and licked up the tree that she and her troop were roosting on for the night. "Aiy, it was too terrible. I got away but mama was not so lucky."

"Did the hot red thing bite your tail?" asked Ntombi.

"Yebo. Yes. These bitey Flies are shoopering me like steric. I wish my Mama was here to groom me. Some of the other mamas just nip me if I get too close."

Giving a little chirp of shock, Tubi thought how strange these hairy Baboons were, so different from his flock. It was so easy for an Oxpecker to rid itself of pests like Flies and Ticks. "Won't someone else do that for you?"

Shaking her head again, Jabu told them how her mother wasn't high enough on the Baboon's social ranks and that Jabu would have to find a higher-ranking mate to climb the social ladder.

Clicking his beak together in a "tsk" sound, Tubi landed on the scrawny Baboon's back towards her infested tail and started pecking at the Flies and their wriggling lava that had already hatched on the festering sores. "I'm not your mama but maybe I can help."

Waiting for Tubi to help their friend, Ntombi sat with Jabu in silence. They were both thinking of all they had lost when a sudden thought occurred to her. "Jabu, you haven't seen Gogo or the crash?"

"Nah. But I'll ask the family."

The troop of Baboons had been softly grunting around them foraging for bugs and seeds, whilst Jabu enjoyed her first grooming in days. When Jabu turned around to ask the troop, she suddenly realised that the softs grunts had fallen silent. "Hey! Where they gone?"

Jabu ran around screaming and barking for the troop. She clambered up several trees and bounded onto boulders, there was no answer. They'd just vanished. Clambering up to the top of a tree, Jabu leaned out hoping to catch sight of them. Hopping back onto Ntombi's large head, Tubi pecked at what looked like a Tick, letting go when he realised that was a piece of Ntombi's skin that had been torn by the Hyena.

"You can stay with us, Jabu. I'll share."

Dropping down from the tree, Jabu sat in the dust and placed her hands on her knees.

"I dunno. What if they come back?"

"They've gone, Jabu. Maybe we can help each other," said Ntombi.

"How can they leave me? You sure I can come with you?"

"Yip, Mama always said it was safer together."

With a sigh, Jabu clambered onto Ntombi's back and took the bite-you gently from Tubi's beak.

"Giddy-up. At least you two won't bite me." She added, "Will you?"

Giving a shake of her head, Ntombi tried to rid herself of the pestering Flies that harassed what was left of her torn and tattered ear.

"We're a pair, aren't we, Jabu? Me with my wonky ear and you with your crooked tail."

The helicopter ride was uneventful. Both teenagers sat staring down at the vastness of the Dwala Safari Park as they flew over it, watching the scenery change from the large monolithic granite rocky formations and valleys to more open grasslands. The vegetation changed too; the small scrubby Acacia bushes gave way to larger Acacias and dotted across the landscape were the strange silhouettes of the majestic ancient Baobab tree, its bare stubby branches reached into the open air looking as if it had been planted upside down and its roots had somehow been stuck into the sky.

Breaking the silence in the cabin of the chopper, Max's voice crackled over the headphones. "They're amazing, aren't they? The Baobab trees. Some call it the tree of life, it's easy to see why experts say they can live for thousands of years."

Then Max pointed to the river in the distance, its rushing waters already visible from the chopper as it forged its way through the African bush, its waters bringing life to the dry arid surroundings.

"There's the Bhavuma river. The bush camp's just under those ebony trees."

Dusty paths snaked towards the river from all directions, Abigail gasped when she spotted the unmistakable grey shape of a lone elephant bull, as it ambled down one of the paths on its way to drink and bathe.

"Why's it called Bhavuma, Max?"

"Means to growl. The river flows north and finally tumbles into the gorge over a hundred feet below. The growling sound the waterfall makes is what gives this river its name."

"Cool. Can't wait to hear that," said Dexter.

"We are too far upstream to hear it. No time to visit the falls this trip. Perhaps another time."

Finding a big enough open space, Max brought the helicopter down with a slight thump and they all clambered out and into the waiting vehicle. Once their overnight bags had been loaded, they drove the short distance to the camp. The bush camp was very different from the Dwala Lodge, it was more rustic with a small thatched central building that was the dining and sitting area. Four olive green dome tents were set up under the lush shady ebony trees. Max had explained that the trees got their names from their dark ebony coloured wood and that its timber is hardy, durable and fairly termite, resistant making it an excellent tree for several uses, and was a prized commodity among ancient traders to Africa. Armed with sundowners, they sat in canvas and wooden directors' chairs, like those you might find on a movie set with the director barking orders. With the Bhavuma river flowing peacefully just a few feet away, the setting sun reflected deeply on its swirling surface making it blush reds and pinks. Now and then a nearby pod of hippos would honk or send a spray of water into the air, not unlike that of a Whale or Dolphin.

Giving a deep sniff, Dexter smelled something familiar, not unlike a smell you might find in a fast-food restaurant.

"Great. Smells like we're having fries for dinner."

Grinning, Max gave a deeply satisfied sniff himself. "Sorry to disappoint you, Dexter. But that potato smell is from a bush, aptly named the potato bush. Its tiny flowers open in the early evening and emit a smell like potatoes or fries."

"It's making me hungry."

A wail of frustration came from Theodore and three heads turned in his direction, to see him staring at his phone in frustration. "No signal."

"Nope. No electricity either. Great, hey!" Max said cheerily.

"No, it bloomin' well isn't."

The next morning, the group of adventurers stood on the banks of the mighty Bhavuma River, three green canoes, with the logo of a Hippo painted on the stern, lay on the soft banks. A woman dressed in what seemed to be the standard uniform amongst the guides and staff—a khaki shirt and shorts—introduced herself as Chipo and briskly started issuing instructions.

"Hi. Max, you'll go with Dexter, in the front

canoe. Theo and Abigail will go in the other canoe together. I'll bring up the rear."

With a nod they all hurriedly followed her directions and stood awaiting her next command. She then started the safety talk. "Occasionally, we get charged by a territorial bull hippo or a mother protecting her calf. Their instinct is to head to deeper water. So, if we run into Hippo, the best thing to do is not get between them and deep water."

On the banks of a small island not far from where they were launching their canoes, Abigail spotted the shape of a Crocodile, its open mouth exposing its sharp glinting white teeth. "What about Crocodiles? Do they attack canoes?"

Following Abigail's pointing hand towards the grinning Crocodile, Max smiled. "Not really, occasionally we startle one off the banks, but they generally avoid us. Fishermen tell a different story though, probably because they gut the fish in the water and the crocs are attracted by the smell of blood."

Once in the canoes, the river rushed beneath them, carrying them downstream. Large birds, the water Dikkops called their "Ti-ti-tee-tee-too" starting fast and then slowing as if they had run out of batteries. On the banks, Baboon and Impala grazed peacefully, barely glancing at the canoeists. Higher up the banks, Elephants crunched on the array of lush greens and the hippo hmphed and honked. Huge colonies of Carmine Bee-eaters, darted out of their riverbank nests, flashing bright pink and blue plumage all the while chittering in alarm.

Giving a great sigh as if a weight had just been lifted from his shoulders, Theodore's paddle rhythmically splashed softly through the water.

"This area is very different from Dwala, isn't it?"

"The river certainly makes a unique environment. Even though it is dry season, there's always lush vegetation for the Elephants. You look like you know what you are doing, Theo. You canoed before?" said Max.

"I did a little when I was in college."

In the front of the canoes, Abigail and Dexter sat occasionally dipping their oars into the water, taking in the vista around them. The Go-Pro had been strapped to Dexter's chest and he clicked it on, the gentle whirr of the camera taking it all in. The pale mauve hills in the distance seemed to frame the river as it forged its way through the escarpment.

Sighing as she took in the surroundings, Abigail pointed at a large bow wave that was rapidly heading in their direction, the size of the wave grew larger as it rippled towards them. "What's that?"

Seeing the massive bow wave heading in their direction, Max slapped his paddle hard on the surface. The sound reverberated across the water.

"Hippo! I lead to the banks. Head to the banks. NOW!"

As fast as he could, Theo put his canoe in reverse and tried to get to the banks of the river. Still, the Hippo pursued their canoe, porpoising out of the water like a Dolphin. As it neared Abi and Theo, its likeness to a Dolphin vanished as it opened its humongous jaws to expose its mammoth teeth, roaring as it went. Behind them, Chipo and Max smacked their oars on the water to distract the roaring animal.

"AAAAARGH! Daddy. It's coming. GO FASTER!" screamed Abigail.

"Listen to me, Abi. Paddle."

Then, as suddenly it had appeared, it turned its immeasurable bulk away from them and with a crashing wave sank beneath the water. Abigail and Theo jumped as their canoe hit the banks behind them with a thump.

Paddling over to them, Max and Dexter looked at their pale faces.

"Are you guys okay?" asked Max.

"That was AWESOME," said Dexter, "You nearly died, and I got it all on camera."

A tear rolled down Abi's cheek, her hands shaking on the paddle. She gasped for breath, ignoring Dexter's callous comment. Seeing how upset Abigail was, Dexter instantly regretted his comment. She wasn't so bad really, this trip he'd seen a kinder, gentler side to her, especially when it came to her passion for the little Rhino. "Sorry, Abs. But you must admit that will definitely impress those toffs at school. Not to mention increase your likes and followers."

"Perhaps we'll stop here for some tea. What do you think, Chipo?" said Max. "That was typical of old Mad Max."

After making sure that the hippo was now a safe distance away, Chipo had now joined them on the riverbank.

Clambering out of his canoe, Dexter looked at Max, impressed. "Mad Max? Is he named after you?"

"Hardly, he's named after that movie. It's our nickname for that Hippo. He's very territorial. Unfortunately, his territory is large, so we never know where he'll be exactly."

Shakily, Abi and Theo get out of their canoe. Abi ran into her father's arms and burst into tears.

Dexter watched them as they hugged and just once he wished either of his parents had hugged him as tightly as Theodore held his daughter now.

The rest of the canoe trip continued with no further incidents and ended just as the sun dipped behind the escarpment, leaving the sky tinged with soft pink hues. They climbed into the waiting safari truck and trundled back towards the bush camp. Once they reached the camp, Theodore announced abruptly that he had a headache and marched off towards his tent.

A sniffle was heard from Abigail's direction as she watched her father retreating.

Turning to walk away, Dexter shook his head. He turned to his stepsister and took her hand, leading her towards the chairs around the fire pit. As they settled into their chairs, Dexter thought that perhaps her life was not as peachy as he thought it was. "Hey, Abs! Let's look at your hippo charge on the laptop. I think there's enough battery left."

After dinner, Max and the staff laid out a picnic-type blanket in front of the fire. He sat down and beckoned the youngsters to join him.

"It's a great spot to do some star gazing and I believe there is a meteor shower tonight. Just remember to cover up and use insect repellent. The Mosquitos here are terrible, you don't want to get malaria."

"What's that?" asked Abigail.

"A meteor shower is a celestial event in which several meteors are observed to radiate or originate from one point in the night sky. These meteors are caused by streams of cosmic debris, called meteoroids, entering the Earth's atmosphere at extremely high speeds on parallel trajectories," replied Dexter.

With a smile, Max looked at the boy. "Did you just swallow an encyclopedia?"

"What's that?"

"Ha. It's a big book of knowledge."

"Oh. Like Wikipedia? That's where I read it."

"But he's right Abi, in a nutshell, we should see lots of shooting stars."

Lying on their backs looking up at the vast dome of twinkling galaxies in front of them, Max pointed out the more prominent constellations of the Milky Way. He showed them the Southern Cross, Sirius the dog star, the aptly named Jewel Box, as well as many other glittering constellations.

"Do you guys know how to find south?"

"Why would we need that? I'll just use Google Earth?" said Dexter.

"Well, Dex, that works, but what if your phone is flat or there's no signal? You just never know what might come in handy one day. It's easy, I even showed it to my son when he was only 6 years old."

Standing in front of Abigail and Dexter, Max showed them four stars that looked a little like a kite. He then showed them another two stars, calling them the pointers, and told them to draw an imaginary line between the pointer stars and another from the foot of the Cross, then draw a third line down to the earth from where the first two lines intersect.

"That should be south or as close as you can get without scientific instruments," said Max.

Dexter rolled his eyes, but did as Max had shown them.

When they had finished, they lay back again, and Max fell silent.

The show began, starting slowly as the first star shot across the deep velvet sky, arching its way gracefully in a bright flash. In a blink it had gone. Abigail and Dexter gasped when another flashed across the dark sky, then another and another. After a while the frequency of the shooting stars seemed to slow and then stopped altogether.

Max got up and went to talk to Chipo and the other bush camp staff.

In a rare moment of comradery, Abigail and Dexter lay on the blanket talking about the last few days and all their experiences. Turning to Abigail, Dexter said quietly, "You're lucky you have your dad, you know."

"He's always working."

"Maybe. But I don't even know where mine is, and I think things aren't going to work out between Theo and my mum."

"What makes you say that?"

"I saw an email from a Divorce lawyer. I didn't see anything more before Theo closed the laptop."

"That's a bummer, Dex. I was just getting used to having you around."

Shrugging, Dexter looked back at the stars.

"Doesn't matter. I wonder where we'll move to next?"

The next morning, Theo announced that Max would be dropping him at the airport so that he could fly back to Johannesburg in South Africa to take care of some business.

"What about us?" asked Dexter.

"You'll go back with Max to Dwala Safari Park."

Her lower lip quivering, Abigail turned her misty eyes to her father. "But Daddy, what about us?"

"I must do this deal. I'll be back before you know it."

"It's not fair. You promised this trip would be different."

"It is unavoidable, Abigail. Maybe Max can organise some riding for you. You'll drop me at the airport, Max?"

Seeing Max's nod, Theo turned on his heel and strode off to finish packing.

Crossing her arms over her chest, Abigail stuck her tongue out at Theo and then stomped off to finish packing her things.

After gaining clearance from Air Traffic Control, Max landed his helicopter on the Chingoma town runway, the nearest city to host an airport that offered direct flights to

Johannesburg. A smartly dressed man greeted them and whisked Theo away to get him cleared through customs and on his way to Johannesburg. Theo nodded curtly to Max, before shoving a fat envelope into his hand, then turned and walked away with a brief wave to the youngsters standing next to Max on the runway.

"Well, guys. Looks like you're stuck with me," said Max.

Giving the sullen children an apologetic smile, Max eased the envelope open to see it brimming with cash. A hastily scribbled note on the front said, 'This will be a good start towards your wildlife foundation. Regards, Theo.'

"I'm sorry. I know you are disappointed your dad left. But he's assured me he will only be a few days."

Shrugging slightly, Abigail sighed. "It's okay, he does it a lot."

"I'll speak to the camp staff about the horses if you want."

"Nah, I don't think I'll ride. It was my therapist's idea anyway."

Frowning slightly, Max looked at the young girl and shook his head. He just couldn't understand why she had made such an abrupt change on the horse riding. "Let's go then. The choppers waiting."

As they approached the helicopter, Dexter pulled Max aside and made sure that Abigail was out of earshot. "I think she's scared to ride."

After dropping his bombshell, Dexter followed Abigail and climbed into the cherry red Bell helicopter, leaving an open-mouthed Max staring after him.

As the helicopter neared Dwala Safari Park, Dexter and Abi eagerly gazed out the windows, just in case they were lucky enough to see the Rhino from the air or perhaps a Zebra or two. As usual, Dexter had the GoPro on and was filming the landscape as it flashed below them.

"They look just like my pony at home, Lightning. Well, except for the stripes."

Glancing at the pretty young girl sitting next to him, trying hard not to be upset by her father's sudden disappearance, Max kept the chopper steady.

"There's a stable at the next lodge. Are you sure you don't want to ride, Abi?"

A voice scoffed from the back seats, as Dexter glanced over at his stepsister. "Probably for the best. Theo and I agree about horses. Dangerous smelly things."

Abigail stuck her tongue out at her stepbrother. "Shut up, Dexter."

Far below, they could make out the granite boulders, sometimes referred to by the locals as whalebacks, as they rose from the ground the same way a whale breaches in the ocean, and the others that were sometimes called castle formations, as they balanced precariously one on top of the other. It was hard from such a high vantage point to make out the distinctive shapes, but they did manage to find the position of the lodge.

"There's the lodge," said Max, "Almost there, kids. Time for a swim I think."

As they climbed out of the airconditioned helicopter a blast of hot air hit them in the face, not unlike that from a hairdryer.

"It's hotter here, after the cool breezes by the river," said Dexter.

"Yes, October is known sometimes as suicide month," said Max.

"It looks drier too," said Abigail.

"They had a little more rain a few days ago but nothing since," replied Max. Aaah, here's the Land Rover to take us back to the lodge."

Giving a little gasp as a thought flooded her head, Abigail grabbed Max by the arm. "I'd nearly forgotten. What happened to the little Rhino? Have they found her?"

"Yeah. What about the mother, too?" Dexter chipped in.

"I meant to mention it earlier. Still no sign of the baby, I'm afraid. I've no idea what happened to the female. I'll try to find out more when we're back at the lodge."

Ntombi: A Rhino's Story

CHAPTER 13

Kicking up small clouds of grey dust, Ntombi trudged through the parched bush with her two unlikely friends, Tubi the feathery brown Oxpecker and Jabu the scruffy scrawny Baboon, both perched upon her back.

It had only been a few days since the fire and Ntombi and her friends were wandering aimlessly through the Dwala Safari Park, searching fruitlessly for the rest of the Rhinos and Gogo, the old matriarch. It had rained again but only a little and the puddles had quickly dried out, leaving the scorched Safari Park thirstier than ever. Shade was hard to find, especially at midday when the heat hummed as the blazing sun sucked all the moisture out of the ground.

"I'm thirsty. I wish Mama were here, she always knew where to drink."

Then a shadow glided across the ground, Ntombi watched as it grew nearer, snorting and huffing. Was it more of those eerie death-waiting flappers, the Vultures that had sat perched by Ntombi and her mother, waiting for them to die?

A sound that they recognized echoed through the balancing granite boulders of the Dwala Safari Park.

"Weeee-ah, I Iyo-hyo-hyo."

The Fish Eagles' cries can be heard from miles away and they are often found near water. With a little snort, Ntombi shouted out, leaping about like her old self trying to get the Eagle's attention.

"Mama's friend, Farai the swim-catcher. Guys, perhaps she can help!"

None of Ntombi's leaping or squeaking or even Jabu's barking seemed to get the Fish Eagles attention, so with a brave chirp Tubi flapped his much smaller wingers towards the soaring Eagle.

From below, Ntombi and Jabu watched as Tubi flapped furiously towards the Fish Eagle, eventually reaching her, and persuading her to peer down towards the waiting Rhino and Baboon. Banking her large wings towards the ground and coming to land on the branch of a thin spindly tree, the Fish Eagle's bulk made the thin branch arc towards the friends on the ground.

Folding her bronze wings at her back, Farai looked down her yellow beak at Ntombi. "Yebo. What you want?"

Looking intently at Ntombi, she glanced around as if expecting to see others around them.

"Oh ho. You're Lindi's little one? Where's she?"

It was the first time that the friends had seen one of these Eagles up close and for a moment, no one spoke, staring at the elegant bird, who even though the branch swayed slightly underweight, remained calm and motionless until she ruffled her feathers. "Well? Where is she?"

With a shake of her head, Ntombi found her voice. "Gone. Mama is gone."

"Gone? Where?"

With a shaky voice, Ntombi told Farai about the fire and the terrifying upright humans that chased them with their death-spitting sticks that seemed to shoot fire, and how she had run after her mother had told her to.

"It was the last time I saw Mama. She told me to find Gogo. Have you seen her?"

"Aiy, Aiy, Aiy. You poor litlle thing. You are too young to be here on your own. I will look, but it been long time since I have seen any of your kind."

The kindly Fish Eagle shook her head sadly once more and took to the sky to aid in the search, crying as she went.

Whilst waiting for Farai to return, Ntombi wandered about, aimlessly grazing at the odd green shoot. Tubi leapt about on her back looking for his favourite Bite-yous, and Jabu had found an old Poo-pile and was busy scratching through it for snacks.

At last, Farai returned, her wing beat strong as she gracefully landed on the same tree as before. "Sorry. Hapana. Nothing. But ask the Stripy or Shaggy beasts."

As she spoke, they could hear the grunting of the Wildebeests as they grazed on the fresh grass. Popping out of Ntombi's trumpet-shaped ear, Tubi flicked the juicy fat Tick into his open beak.

"Thank you, Farai."

The three friends turned away from the Eagle toward the Wildebeest and Zebra, but Farai called them back.

"Basop, beware. Those deadly Uprights with Firesticks are near. I wish I could help more but I have my babies."

The trio watched as Farai's shadow got smaller and smaller. Ntombi shrugged and plodded in the direction of the Wildebeests. But before they reached them, a smell filled Ntombi's wide nostril, a welcome smell. A cool, wet, and inviting smell,

"Water!" Ntombi exclaimed. "Tubi, I smell water."

They spun in the direction of the smell, the thought of a cool drink invigorating the thirsty trio. Trotting along, Ntombi's nose high in the air, they didn't notice the thin silver strand that lay coiled on the ground until it was too late. It wrapped itself around Ntombi's front leg and she fell onto her nose with a thud, flinging Jabu to the ground and Tubi flapping into the sky.

"Hey!" Jabu said, clambering to his feet.

Eyes wide, Ntombi kicked her foot and tried to get to her feet. The more she struggled, the more the wire tightened its hold on her, adding to her panic.

"I'm stuck. Get it off me."

Seeing Ntombi's fear heightening and that her struggles weren't helping, Jabu indicated to Tubi to help calm the terrified young Rhino.

"Calm down, Ntombi. Let me help."

Looking at the silver strands of wire that wound themselves around Ntombi's foot, he chose a single strand and tugged at it. He tugged and tugged, then with a twang, Ntombi was free. All three sat where Ntombi had fallen and stared at the strange thing as it lay coiled on the ground. Their eyes followed it along the ground as it rose towards a post, and then onto another and another, joining others that formed a fence snaking into the distance.

With a short bark, Jabu turned away from the fence. "I've been here before. It is not safe. We must go back."

"Jabu's right, Ntombi. Let's go," said Tubi.

"But the wet stuff. It is so close," replied Ntombi.

Once again, she lifted her nose and walked off in the direction of the waterhole.

Her two friends looked at each other, knowing that once Ntombi had made up her mind there was little they could do to change it. Looking nervously behind them, they hurriedly followed her.

As the smell grew stronger, the vegetation changed from the dusty and thorny acacia scrub to dense dark green. Pushing through the shrubs, the smell of fresh clean water filled Ntombi's nostrils with intoxicating aromas. Life seemed to sprout all around her with ferns and young palm trees. With a final push, Ntombi clambered through the bush and found a waterhole unlike any she had ever seen. From where she was standing it seemed to flow through the landscape as if it were desperately trying to split it in half. Ntombi stood on the top of a small cliff and the river flowed underneath her, as a flash of bright pink and bluebirds flapped in front of Ntombi, crying out in alarm.

"Oh! It's amazing," said Ntombi.

Glancing around her, Ntombi spotted a well-worn path leading down to the river's edge, and she broke into an eager trot, her head filled with the smell of water. Panting to catch up with the excited Rhino, Tubi just managed to flap down onto the ground in front of her.

"Slow down, Ntombi. Didn't your mother tell you to be careful?"

"I agree. There are strange creatures that lurk in these waters," said Jabu.

But it was too late. Ntombi rushed to the edge of the water and leapt in. Jabu had just enough time to leap off her back onto the ground. With the water lapping under her belly, Ntombi drank and drank and drank. The water was cool and fresh and tasted delicious.

With her nose still in the water, Ntombi noticed something in the water, coming straight toward her. "What's that?"

Nearby, Tubi was enjoying a bath in the

shallows. He fluttered over quickly when he heard Ntombi's little squeak of alarm. They looked at it closely. It moved gracefully and effortlessly through the water, shimmering with each movement.

"How pretty. Jabu, is it a swimmer?"

"Dunno," replied Jabu.

He had drunk his fill and was busy scratching through a strange round object, sending bits flying, eagerly picking up dark red seeds. Still watching as the fish flicked in and out of the water reeds, Ntombi turned to Tubi, who had also moved away from the water and was thinking that it was time he dived under Ntombi's tail again in search of tasty Ticks.

"What do you think, Tubi?"

"I reckon it is," said Tubi.

With a shrug, Ntombi continued drinking when she noticed something else drifting slowly towards them. It looked rather like a log, but Ntombi had never seen a log that floated in that way, especially considering the strong current of the river. All the other logs seemed to be in a hurry, flowing downstream.

"Is that a shade-giver stump? Why is it coming towards me?"

Abandoning his thoughts of a meal, Tubi had flown to a nearby bush and was busy preening himself, when he looked up in alarm. From his perch, he could see the dark green shape of the crocodile as it homed in on Ntombi.

"Ntombi! Watch out!"

Leaping back with start, Ntombi snorted, just in time as the crocodile boiled out of the water, its scary sharp teeth snapping after her.

"What-was-that? I don't like it. Too snappy."

"Me either. It looked hungry," agreed Tubi.

From the safety of a tree, Jabu chittered nervously.

"One got Great-Uncle Wally. He was drinking at the side of a waterhole, and the next minute there was an almighty splash and Uncle Wally was gone."

"Just gone?" said Tubi.

"Yup! Snap. Gone," replied Jabu, clapping his hands together to emphasize the teeth of the crocodile. Then he continued, "Gave me nightmares for ages and Mother used it to get me to listen afterwards, threatening me that it was behind me, watching. I can still imagine its mouth and its wide toothy grin."

"It wasn't big enough to eat me," stated Ntombi.

"Maybe not but those things looked sharp. I think we should find somewhere safe for the dark time," said Tubi.

"This is a dangerous place at dark time," agreed Jabu with a shudder.

After some discussion, the trio decided that perhaps it would be best to stick to the hidden valleys amongst the giants.

"But which way do we go?" asked Ntombi, looking around.

Next to Ntombi, Jabu stood scratching an itchy bit on his bottom.

"Well, we followed that large path down to the flowing waterhole, why not follow it back again?"

With a nod, Ntombi turned towards the large path, in the middle of it was still a large round pile of dung, with an excited squeak Ntombi ran up to it, certain that it would tell her that another Rhino was nearby. She stuck her nose onto the pile and inhaled deeply. Scrunching up her nose in disgust, when she realised that this dung pile was not made by a Rhino.

"Yuck! What made this? It is not Lumber beast."

A little peck from Tubi, who was perched between her ears.

"Ah. Ntombi. I think we should go," said Tubi.

"Why?"

Then Ntombi saw it. A massive grey shape towered over her, its trunk reaching high into a tree, casually ripping branches off the dark green tree as if it were nothing but a twiglet. The wrinkled trunk stuffed the dark green leaves and bits of branch into his open mouth, two great ivory tusks glinting in the sunlight. Backing away from the elephant as quietly as they could, Ntombi and her friends turned up the path and ran. The Elephant turned towards them slightly when the movement caught the corner of his eye, and with a soft snort he ignored them and continued with his meal.

"What was that?"

Looking over his shoulder, Jabu tried to stop his

shaking legs and gave a little shrug, trying to appear his usual cheeky self. "Angazi. Don't know. But it was huge."

Creeping out from behind Ntombi's ears, Tubi's eyes opened, and he breathed a huge sigh. "Let's get outta here before it follows us."

Nodding, Ntombi turned away from the river back in the direction they had come, casting one last glance towards the tree where they had last seen the Elephant. It had disappeared without a sound, leaving the remains of his meal scattered on the ground, and the tree in shreds. Putting her head down, Ntombi waited for Jabu to settle on her back as usual, and for Tubi to get comfortable on his perch between her ears. She trudged down the track, dust puffing at her feet.

In the distance, unseen by the trio, a helicopter was briefly silhouetted by the sun as it rose above the river and flew over the horizon.

Abigail and Dexter made their way to the dining room at the Dwala Lodge, droplets of water still dripping from their hair after a refreshing dip in the pool.

A tantalizing aroma filled the air and Dexter's stomach answered with a deep rumble, causing Max to chuckle as he came up behind them. "There's a hungry Lion nearby."

Smiling and ducking his head slightly, Dexter's cheeks turned a pale pink. "When's dinner?"

"Is that all you think about? Your stomach?" said Abigail.

"Won't be too long, Dexter. No news about the Rhino I'm afraid. The game scouts are anxious for extra help if you two are willing. We could take a drive tomorrow morning," said Max.

Two eager faces turned towards Max both nodding vigorously.

Dexter gave a great sigh as the evening's hog roast was carried into the dining room, his eyes widening. "Finally. Let's eat!"

During dinner, Abigail and Dexter pestered Max with questions about the news of the Rhino.

"Is the female Rhino still alive?" said Abigail.

"Can the baby survive without her?"

"Slow down, guys. No idea about the female, last I heard she was taken to the vet clinic. You remember Dr Ben, sadly he is always kept very busy. He may be out saving other wildlife; they work with all wildlife, not just Rhinos. Poachers don't seem to rest."

"What about the baby though?" asked Dexter.

"A baby Rhino needs her mother, but there have been rare cases of other mothers adopting an orphaned baby. There is another female with a young calf. It's a long shot but we can hope, hey?"

Shoving his dessert spoon in his mouth, Dexter hastily swallowed the gooey chocolate mousse, waving frantically at Max. "I got some interesting footage today, Max. Can I show it to you?"

"Ja. Let's have a look."

Pointing at the screen, Dexter showed Max and Abigail what he had filmed from the helicopter.

"There. What's that?"

He paused the film on a scene from the start of their trip. The river was just seen in the background and the distinctive shape of an Elephant reached its trunk up to pull leaves from a tree. A little distance from the elephant was a smaller grey shape. The image was a little fuzzy, but the shape was unmistakable.

Gasping, Abigail touched the screen. "Is that the little Rhino?"

CHAPTER 14

Trudging along, Ntombi and her friends barely noticed as the sky turned from brilliant blue to shades of magenta and pink, and finally indigo. The sounds of Cape Turtle Doves faded away, replaced by trilling Nightjars and the eerie screeches of Owls. On the horizon stood the towering granite boulders silhouetted against the inky darkness of the twinkling dome above them.

Darkness found the young Rhino, the scruffy Baboon and the dusky brown bird hidden amongst the flecked grey granite giant boulders.

The three friends had found a small patch of green swishy grassy snacks and Ntombi tried to eat, even if it was just to make her friends happy. Eventually, Ntombi lay under a spindly silver-leafed tree, Tubi perched on her head. Not feeling comfortable, Jabu leapt nimbly into the branches above and they chatted for a little until they all fell into an exhausted sleep. As Ntombi's eyes closed, she remembered the warmth of her mother as they lay cuddled together; all she wanted was to suckle her mother and breathe in her comforting musky smell. Overhead, the clouds darkened and obscured the stars completely.

None of them noticed the distant rumble or the flashes of light that lit up their hiding place. The rumbling grew closer and closer until—with a crash and a bolt of blinding light—it was directly above them. Jabu, who was still perched above, gave a startled squeal and then—*plop, plop, plop*—he loosened his bowels right onto Ntombi, who was directly underneath.

Leaping to her feet, Ntombi wailed at the Baboon who still sat in the tree above sheepishly grinning at her. "Hey! What's that smell?"

"Sorry. I pooed."

Rolling in the grass, feet in the air, Ntombi tried to rid herself of the offensive smell that lingered in her nostrils. "Jabu! Gross!"

Tubi, who had managed to escape being splattered, looked at Ntombi and although he tried to keep it in, burst out laughing. "Pffst. Hahaha," he chortled, "you should see your face, Ntombi."

Then they were all laughing. They rolled about and Ntombi chased Jabu as he howled with laughter, their troubles temporarily forgotten. Seeing that they were all awake, they thought that perhaps they should get going. So, they followed the narrow track deeper into the rocky crevice, as the flashes of lightning and rumbling thunder rolled away into the distance.

Suddenly, Ntombi gave an excited shriek, a familiar smell filled her nostrils. "Guys! Look! A poo-pile. Or at least it smells like one. It's been scattered all over the place."

"Anyone we know?" asked Tubi.

Placing her wide square snout on the scattered dung, bits of chewed sticks and leaves protruded from the matted contents. With a deep breath, Ntombi sucked in the scent, wrinkling her wide nose, trying to figure out who it belonged to.

"It's a Lumber-beast but it's different."

Leaping off her back, Jabu hungrily attacked the pile, looking for snacks of Dung Beetle or bits of seeds.

"Let's follow the smell and see if it can help," said Jabu.

Nodding, Ntombi breathed in again and they followed the scent winding through a deep gorge, the granite giants surrounding them as the darkness turned slowly lighter, and another new day dawned.

Ntombi looked around her with interest, she had never been to this area before. The crash had always preferred the more open plains to these crevices amongst the granite rocky giants. Even the trees looked different, no spines or sharp thorns. They clung to the walls of granite, cream-coloured roots snaking down the mottled grey rock, looking like they were strangling the very life out of the rocks.

Small eyes seemed to dart in and out of the crevices, causing Jabu to give a little shudder. Her mother had once told her a story of a spotted beast, a leopard, that hid amongst the rocks. "I don't like it here. Something's watching."

No sooner had she said that a small nose appeared from a crack in the rock. It peered down at them through small bright black eyes, its plump brownish-grey furry body blending perfectly with its surroundings. Giving a screech, Jabu clambered up a nearby strangler fig, causing the little creature to dart back into the dark hole.

With a flutter, Tubi flew from Ntombi's head to the rock and peered into the darkness. "Don't be such a baby, Jabu."

The nose of the fuzzy brown Hyrax reappeared and before the others could respond or greet the little creature it darted off again and was gone.

"What was that? I hope we didn't frighten it," said Ntombi.

Slowly, Jabu slid down the tree and stood squinting into a small cave in the rock, absently scratching his butt with one hand.

"It's a rock-dweller. They're very shy."

"It's gone now," said Tubi.

With a leap, Jabu landed on Ntombi's rump and Tubi fluttered onto the top of her head, looking eagerly at her torn and tattered ear.

"Tons of Bite-yous in your ears."

Shaking her head as Tubi's voice chirped inside her head, Ntombi tried to dislodge her friend, who flew into the air with an annoyed twitter.

"Not now, Tubi. Wait. What's that?"

Nearby they heard the distinctive call of another Oxpecker; surely this could mean only one thing. The Rhino crash. They had found them.

Bils of Tick and other critters flew out of his beak as Tubi flapped and chirped. He had spotted a large steely grey backside, the dense dark green vegetation scraping against his side. The creature grazed on the bush in front of him, his prehensile lip helping to tug at the twigs.

"Hey! Over here."

There was a loud snort as the other Rhino suddenly spotted them. He turned and charged, not waiting to find out if they were friend or foe.

Bushes exploded as he forged his way through them, huffing and puffing like a steam train, dust flying.

Screaming from on top of Ntombi's back, Jabu clung on like a racehorse jockey.

"GO! RUN! He's not stopping."

Not needing any encouragement, Ntombi jumped back on the narrow path and fled away from the angry black Rhino with the sharp pointy horn. Ntombi didn't stop until they burst out of the rocky crevice and into open grasslands, though by then the cantankerous animal had given up, satisfied that he had seen off his unwelcome visitors.

Catching up to his friends Tubi flapped onto the ground and tried to settle his ruffled feathers. "Phew, it's gone. Why did it chase us?"

"My mama talked of another like Ntombi. She said it's grumpy because it is alone." said Jabu.

Thumping down on her bottom, causing Jabu to slide off in a tangle of legs and arms, Ntombi gave a little sniff.

"I no like the grumpy Lumber-beast. I thought it was Mama or Gogo."

"Aiy. Sorry, my friend. That was too scary," said Tubi.

"Eh, he. Too scary and it ate sticks. Not swishy snack, like you Ntombi," said Jabu.

The granite rock surface dwarfed the young teenagers and their guide as they stood next to its monolithic mass staring through the rocks and crevices, trying to see where the dusty path went. Lichens of luminous yellows, greens and amber clung to the rocks' surfaces, making the dull grey surface look more like an artist's canvas than something nature created.

Touching a patch of lemon-yellow lichen, Abigail's fingers traced the rough surface. "Who messed paint here, Max?"

"It's lichen, Abi. It's a slow-growing plant, or more accurately, the symbiotic relationship of a fungus and an algae. It certainly creates a vibrant scenery, hey."

Unimpressed, Dexter scoffed and then followed the track as it led between the boulders of all shapes and sizes jutting out in all directions, the pale white trees clinging to the rocks as if they might blow away. "We have to go in there?"

"Yup. The Rangers said it was worth checking out as they hadn't managed to search in here themselves yet."

Shrugging, Abigail gestured with her hand towards the track. "Lead on, Max."

"Shhh. Let's go quietly."

They followed Max as he led them into the crevices between the balancing boulders. The vegetation changed, with strange and unusual trees so different from the Silver-leafed Terminalia and Acacia's that they had seen on the open plains.

Passing a dark grey boulder, Abigail ran her hands along with the smooth creamy roots of a tree that seemed to squeeze the life out of the rock.

"What a strange tree."

Reaching out to trace the path of the root, Max smiled at the girl. "It's a Strangler Fig. The roots of this tree have been known to split the rocks over time."

Behind them came a hum from the GoPro attached to Dexter's chest. He was hardly ever without it since Max had loaned it to him days ago. "Wicked. A sinister tree. Mates back home won't believe this."

Chuckling at Dexter's comment, Max turned away from the tree and commented over his shoulder. "It is. All in the search of water."

Glancing back down towards the ground, Max's eyes darted left and right, whilst he searched for the tell-tale signs wildlife may have passed through the valley. He paused for a moment, leaning closer to the ground. "Hook-lipped Rhino spoor. Look!"

Pointing to the ground, Max lightly traced the track with his finger, creating a more defined outline for his young guests.

"What's a hook-lipped Rhino?" asked Abi. "Is it different to the white Rhino we've seen?"

Shaking his head, Max explained the differences between the two Rhino species found in the Safari Park.

"It's the correct name for a Black Rhino.

People mainly refer to the two African species of Rhino as black and white, but they are both a shade of grey and whatever the colour of the mud they have rolled in. Some think that there was a misunderstanding, when the first English-speaking settlers arrived in Africa, the Dutch referred to it as a 'Wiet' Rhino. It was mistaken for white. When it meant wide. So, when the smaller cousin was spotted, they called it black."

"That's so stupid," said Dexter.

Turning and pasting a broad smile on her face, Abigail said into the GoPro camera, "Idiots. Have we seen any Black Rhino?"

"No, not yet but this is prime territory for them."

Suddenly, a face peered out at them from a rocky ledge and before anyone could react it darted away. Stopping, Max put his fingers to his lips, and they waited for a short while, a little button nose, followed by small bright black eyes and a brown fuzzy body about the size of a large guinea pig appeared. It cocked its head to one side. They looked at each other for a split second, then it was gone.

"A Rock Hyrax."

Clasping her hands to her face, Abigail squealed as she investigated the crevice where the Hyrax had disappeared. "So cute. I want one."

Hearing that, Dexter rolled his eyes and shrugged at the camera, before giving her a slight shove to follow Max, who had walked off around the bend in the path. This caused Abigail to stumble over a root sticking out of the ground.

"Hey!"

Dropping his voice to an urgent whisper, Max turned to them. "Quiet! I hear something."

Ahead of them came the tell-tale sign of an Oxpecker, crying out its warning, then a SNORT and the crashing of something big moving fast through the dense bushes.

Wasting no time, Max pushed and shoved Abigail and Dexter, as the snorting beast thundered towards them. "Up here!"

Grabbing both Abi and Dexter by the arms, Max manhandled them up a nearby Strangler Fig. He was still clambering up the tree when a large Rhino boiled towards him, ramming the closest tree. The tree groaned and shuddered under the force of the attack. Catching sight of Max, the Rhino turned his attention towards them and the tree in which they had clambered. Sucking his rear end up into the tree with the dexterity of a Baboon, Max's bottom was only inches from the sharp pointed horn. The three of them reached up onto the overhanging boulder, as the large Rhino charged underneath. It stopped, peered round and with a final snort trotted off in the other direction.

Running a hand shakily through his hair, Dexter let out a long breath. "Oh my god. That was so wicked."

Grinning Max turned to look at the pale faces of the pair next to him. "You guys, okay? He certainly showed us who was boss, hey."

Two heads nodded back in unison.

"Let's get back to the truck. I think that's enough excitement for today."

Recovering first, Dexter cleared his throat as if not trusting his voice. "Was that a hook-lipped Rhino? It looked grumpy."

"It was. Well done, Dex. Did you see the difference in his mouth? Something must have disturbed it."

Licking his finger and holding it up to test the wind direction, Max shook his head. "It wasn't us; the wind direction was perfect."

They clambered shakily down the rock. Retracing their steps, they hurriedly headed back to the truck. Abi and Dexter's eyes darted around them, worried that it might come back. They saw the truck as soon as they burst into the clearing, and hurriedly climbed in and thumped down in the seat at the back. Max went to the back to get them all drinks.

Already it was so hot that Abigail could feel the sweat trickling down between her shoulder blades, she fanned her face with her hand and reached into her bag to pull out a small mirror, checking her makeup was still in place, muttering when she saw her ruddy-faced and smeared reflection. "Oh god. Look at me."

Grinning, Dexter turned the little camera in her direction, the tell-tale red light flicking as the camera filmed the flustered girl.

"Ha-ha. Abi, say hi to your followers."

Trying to grab the camera from Dexter's outstretched hand, Abigail wrestled and tugged to no avail. Eventually she let out a piercing scream, "Nooooo."

Running around the side of the truck, Max's concerned face appeared, the cooler box forgotten in his haste to protect his young guest. He heaved a heavy sigh and glared at Dexter, who reluctantly switched the camera off and put it down.

"Oh okay. Fine. But I'm still posting the Rhino charge. Will be good to show the viewers the difference between the Rhinos."

Nodding curtly at the boy, Max retrieved the cooler box and placed it carefully into the back of the truck. He handed drinks to the two of them and climbed into the driver's seat. Starting the engine and giving the kids the thumbs up, he put it in gear and was just about to reverse when he spotted a figure walking out of the valley. Slowly, Max's hand reached for the rifle that was stored in its usual place on the dash of the vehicle, breathing a sigh of relief when the man stepped out of the shadows

255

to reveal the olive-green uniform of the Safari Park Rangers.

Leaning out of the driver's seat, Max greeted the man with the usual African handshake, a series of hand pumps and thumb clasping. The man was young and full of enthusiasm as he spoke rapidly to Max in the local language, Ndebele.

Jumping out of the truck, Max retrieved another drink from the back and handed it to the Ranger who in turn downed the drink in one gulp and handed the empty bottle back to Max. Then with a cheery wave, the young Ranger turned and walked off, back in the direction he had come.

In the back, Dexter and Abigail had tried to follow the conversation and they turned on Max.

Abigail was the first to speak. "What was that about?"

"Yeah. Come on. Spill it, Max."

"Well, it seems that the Ranger was following tracks of what he thought was a young white Rhino when he heard all the sorting and what have you. I think we weren't the only thing that Black Rhino sent packing."

"Is it the lost baby?" asked Abigail.

"It could be. The Ranger has asked me to notify the head Ranger and said he will try to find the tracks again. All the tracks have been trampled on by either us or the black Rhino."

"Oh, let's hope it's her," said Abigail.

"Come to think of it, there's a cave not too far from here. Has some great rock paintings from those San people I mentioned. It also has a great view."

"Those San people are the ones that lived in these hills hundreds and possibly thousands of years ago, isn't that right?" said Dexter.

Ntombi: A Rhino's Story

CHAPTER 15

After their near-miss with the territorial hook-lipped black Rhino, Ntombi and her friends wandered about the open grassy plains, Jabu and Tubi trying to get Ntombi to eat a little of the yellowing swishy grass, faintly tinged with green. Even the short rainfall had bought new life and hope to the Dwala Safari Park. To make her friends happy, Ntombi nibbled a little grass here and there, as she had seen her mother do, but she was still too young to be without her mother's nourishing milk.

A snort from behind a nearby bush startled Ntombi and she shied away from the sound, spraying a shower of dirt as she spun away. It snorted again, and a glossy grey-brown shape appeared behind the bearded face of a Wilde-beest, peering around the bush.

"Gnu"

Gambolling towards the Wildebeest, Ntombi called over her shoulder to Jabu who was busy scratching through the dirt and Tubi who hopped about her back.

"Guys! Shaggy-beasts!"

Without waiting for a response from Jabu or Tubi, Ntombi rushed over to the spindly Wildebeest, who looked up at her with a blank expression on its face.

"Hi! Have you seen my family?"

"Gnee, Gnu."

Oh, not this again, thought Ntombi, remembering her last fruitless conversation with one of these beasts. She looked at Tubi and then to Jabu helplessly, they both shrugged and returned to their important task of foraging for food. With her cheeks crammed full of mahogany-coloured berries, Jabu tried to ram in yet another, his voice muffled as he spoke.

"What about Dube the stripy beast? Don't they move together?"

From the back of the Wildebeest, Tubi gave a little flutter knowing that Jabu was right; the Zebra and Wildebeest were often seen together.

"Good idea! These Shaggy things are useless, except for Bite-yous."

With a faint sigh and a shake of her head, Ntombi looked towards Jabu who had managed to finish his mouthful and was now flicking through a dusty bowl, in pursuit of yet another snack.

"Is that all you think about, Tubi?"

After a little persuading, Tubi the Oxpecker and Jabu the Baboon, gave up their food search and followed Ntombi, in search of Dube, the Zebra. They hadn't gone far when they spotted him, grazing with a group of other Zebras and Wildebeests, sounds of munching and soft contented snorts.

"Hey, Dube!" called Tubi.

The trilling warning cry of the little dusky-brown Oxpecker startled the Zebra, and they took off at a gallop, in a blur of stripes, thus startling the Shaggy-beasts until there was a jumble of stripes and lolloping knobbly legs.

"Oops. Maybe one of you should call him."

Ntombi slowly approached the jumble of stripes. The Zebra stood together, snorting and stamping their hooves, and Ntombi strained to spot Dube through the throng of stripes. Finally, Ntombi spotted him, standing alongside his mother, their stripes mingling together. "Dube, it's me, Ntombi. We need your help."

Stepping away from the protective stripey illusion, Dube breathed a sigh of relief when he spotted his bedraggled Rhino friend. "Ntombi? You scared the stripes off us. Whadda matter?"

They told Dube all that had happened and asked if he had seen the crash of Rhino. The little Zebra stood with his mother and listened, shaking his head as he took in the devastating story.

"Aiy, that is too terrible."

Turning towards his mother, who stood just behind Dube keeping a watchful eye on her foal.

It was the Zebra mare who spoke up. "Sorry for your trouble, little one. We have seen some big lumber beasts like you. Just past those rocky Giants, but that was—"

With a squeak, Ntombi gave a burst of energy, interrupting the mare. She broke into a lumbering trot towards the giant granite boulder. "Let's go!"

"Wait! Ntombi! Basop! It is too dangerous!"

The Zebra mare and her son Dube tried to call the Rhino back to finish what she had started to tell them. In the end, they gave up as they watched the retreating rump of the little Rhino swagger off through the tawny grasses.

"Aiy, Dube. That one is too hasty. Let us hope she avoids the danger that chased away the others."

Unaware that the Rhino crash had already gone, the young calf and her friends rushed towards where they were certain that they would finally find Gogo, the old matriarch of the Rhino herd.

Spindly thorny bushes and scratchy reeds scraped Ntombi's grey wrinkled hide as she forged her way through the vegetation, no regard for her friends who struggled to keep up with her. It was not an area that any of the animals recognized, and it worried Tubi, who struggled to see Ntombi as she pushed her way through the grasses and reeds of an ancient river course that had flowed many centuries ago amongst the jutting granite boulders.

"Slow down, Ntombi! Be careful!"

But Tubi's objections fell on deaf ears as Ntombi tore off without checking for dangers, squeaking as she skidded around the rocks and into the open plains on the other side.

"Gogo!"

Only the cackle of a few helmeted Guineafowls as they sprinted away from Ntombi, their spotty grey-blue plumage flouncing like old women's skirts above their scrawny yellow chicken-like legs. But where were Gogo and the Rhino crash?

Rushing about, Ntombi went across the open plains, searching behind every bush until Jabu gave a little leap and pointed at a familiar lump of dung.

It shifted and transformed as the Dung Beetles went about their work, chomping and rolling it into balls. "Look! They were here."

Fluttering down onto the top of Jabu's head, Tubi stared at the heaving mass, as Jabu the Baboon dug out a wriggling plump shiny iridescent Dung Beetle and popped it in his mouth with a crunch.

"Gone now! Let's—"

A thin wail emitted from the little Rhino. Tubi looked at Ntombi in astonishment, as she flopped onto the dusty ground in a heap of wrinkled skin and bones. Her sunken eyes stared at the dung pile in front of her. "It's hopeless. We'll never find her."

Hopping onto the front of her face, near her stubby horn, Tubi laid his tiny feathered head on hers. "Aiy! No! Don't give up. We'll find her."

"I'm tired."

Placing his hands on either side of Ntombi's face, as her eyelids slid closed, Jabu stroked her face, whispering soothingly. "Come on Ntombi, don't give up now."

Sitting next to her drooping torn ear, still oozing, and attracting Flies, Tubi noticed a big fat juicy Tick on her eyelid. He hopped down her thick wrinkled face and pecked at it. Ntombi just gave a quick flick of her ear and puffed out a gaff of air through her wide nostrils. Tubi gave a frustrated chirp. "Oh! You talk to her, Jabu."

Deciding it was time to get tough, Jabu raised her voice and stopped stroking Ntombi's face, poking her long thin finger on the top of her snout. "You listen to me, Ntombi. Lindi would not want you to give up, she sacrificed everything for you. Now, move."

Softening a little, Jabu looked at her friend and shook her head, she was still only a baby after all. "I've lost a mama too and I miss her also. But we have each other. Now, come on."

Huffing, Ntombi's large nostrils caused a puff of dust to fly into the Baboon's face and she spluttered, wiping the dust from her piercing orange eyes.

"Sorry, Jabu. I know that you've lost your mama and troop too."

"That's it, Ntombi," said Tubi.

Chirping encouragingly, Tubi flapped off in front of her leading the way out of the plains, away from the disappointing pile of Rhino dung.

Clambering slowly to her feet, Ntombi placed one wobbly foot in front of the other and plodded after Tubi as Jabu gambolled after them both.

Later, they stopped for a rest under a suitable shady tree, which was covered in dark green leaves, not unlike Gogo's favourite tree in the territory.

Jabu was scratching about in the dirt hoping to find a tasty treat, perhaps a bug or two, or even a nut or seed. Tubi hopped about on Ntombi, pecking at her Ticks. After he had had his fill, he flew over to Jabu, who had now clambered up a silvery Terminalia tree and was picking at its purple pods.

"I'm worried about her. She's too skinny. Jabu, how'd you cope without a Mama?"

Shrugging, Jabu scrutinized a purple pod and then popped it in her mouth. "Not good to dwell on the past."

Jabu picked up another seedpod and popped it in her mouth, chomping it thoughtfully.

"Besides, Ntombi is a baby and needs her mama. I'm old enough and don't need my Mama."

"Aiy. Jabu. It is not good."

Shrugging Jabu continued to root out the seed pods that had fallen on the ground at the base of a small tree.

"It's okay. Long as there is stuff to scoff at. Besides, I have you two."

A few hours later, Max, Abigail and Dexter stood on top of a Whaleback Dwala or Kopje as it was called locally, the domed grey granite boulder looking like an artist's palette splashed with bright vibrant ambers, lime-greens, and lemon-yellow lichen. It felt as if they were standing on top of the world. A herd of Zebra and Wildebeest grazed in the golden grasses below, although they were best seen through a good pair of binoculars.

Panting, Dexter clutched his aching sides.

"When you said a hike, you didn't say that the hike was almost all up."

Standing next to her stepbrother, Abigail was busy pushing strands of loose hair back into her ponytail. Taking her little mirror out of her tiny Gucci backpack, she checked her glowing red face and applied a little powder. "Stop whining, Dexter. It wasn't that bad."

"Not all of us are on the track team, you know," said Dexter, still huffing.

Smiling, Max turned away from the bickering youngsters, knowing that it was exactly what siblings did, and stared into the mouth of the cave.

"It certainly gets the heart rate going."

Finally catching their breath, Dexter and Abigail joined Max at the arch of the cave mouth. Its huge yawn exposed a dome-shaped bubble inside the granite rock, and on the walls were rustic paintings of animals and smaller versions of what looked like stick men carrying spears.

Gesturing to the inverted cathedral-like dome, Max diverted the children's attention from their argument.

"This is the Tondolo cave. It is one of the larger caves in the area and the painting are some of the oldest in the world."

With his eyes still searching the roof of the cave, Max pointed out various paintings of Giraffes, Wildebeest and even a Rhino.

"I may have said before that these formations were formed bilLions of years ago when the granite was pushed up through the surface then carved by many years of weathering. These rocks have been home to many, including stone age man, but the ones that left behind these paintings are the bushmen or San people."

The paintings stood out against the grey rock in shades of amber, reds, and yellows. They adorned the cave like wallpaper.

A faint hum reminded Max that Dexter was filming him as he talked. Turning to look out through the cave mouth, they could almost see when the horizon dipped its arch downwards, confirming that the earth was indeed round.

"They certainly had an amazing view. You can see for miles from here."

"A perfect place to see what's on the menu."

Abigail was wandering around the cave, looking at the paintings, when she cast her eyes downwards. She spotted a boot print in the powdery dust on the cave floor and in a corner sat a pile of logs that looked like the remains of a fire. "Max? Did the Bush people make fires?"

With a start, Max turned back to Abigail and stared in shock at the fire. He placed his hand over it to feel the faint warmth that radiated from the ashes. "That's not from bushmen, Abi. It's still warm. We need to go now."

Suddenly, Dexter shouted. "Max, what's that down there?"

Rushing over to the edge, where Dexter stood pointing down into the dry sandy valley below, several shapes were moving along an old track, dust trailing faintly behind them. Putting his binoculars to his face Max, peered down at the shapes. "It's a young Rhino."

With a squeak, Abigail grabbed the binoculars from Max trying to get a better look. "Is it the lost baby?"

"It could be. We need to contact the Rangers. Let's get back now."

Already Max had his old, battered Nokia out of his pocket and was holding it high in the air. "Blast! No signal."

Another shout, this time from Abigail. "Wait! What's that?"

The young girl was pointing to a more upright-like shape that lurked in shadows some distance from the little Rhino, she passed the binoculars to Max. "Is it that Ranger we saw earlier?"

"We need to get back to the lodge now."

"Why? What's wrong?"

The question came from Dexter, as he trotted behind Max, who was already striding away from them down the side of the granite kopje. Turning to bark at the kids who were trailing behind, he wiped a shaky hand over his face. He thought of the man in the shadows, the sunlight just glinting off the barrel of his rifle, as he held it loosely in his hands.

"Hurry up!"

"But—"

Still full of questions, Dexter and Abigail were at a loss for words at being spoken to so harshly. They had stopped and were staring at Max's rapidly retreating form, their mouths agape.

In two long strides, Max turned back, and the youngsters jumped when he barked again. "A poacher with a rifle. Now! Move!"

Needing no further encouragement, Dexter and Abigail slid and scrambled their way down the steep kopje and raced for the Land Rover. Wasting no time, Max jumped into the driver's seat and quickly checked that his young charges were safely seated in the back. The vehicle lurched forwards as Max slammed his foot on the accelerator.

Dust billowed behind the Land Rover as it screeched into the lodge's carpark, Max leapt out, shouting for the camp staff, as he took the steps two at a time. He reached the top and stopped.

"Come on, you two. Hurry up. We need to tell the Rangers where to look for that baby Rhino."

Two pairs of wide eyes blinked back at Max, both youngsters still clinging to the Land Rover seats. Running a shaky hand through her tousled hair, Abigail was the first to recover. She clambered down the small ladder of steps that ran up the side of the truck. Her legs gave way a little when she reached the bottom, and she placed a hand on the truck side to steady herself. "That was a bit fast, Max."

"Ja. Sorry. Look, I'll see you both in the dining area for lunch. Okay?"

He turned and half walked half-ran, still yelling for the lodge manager.

Joining Abigail on the ground, Dexter gave a shaky sigh. "Let's get a soda."

"Yeah. One full of sugar."

A few minutes later, Vusa the lodge manager, walked in just as the young guests were getting their drinks. The cool sparkling liquid bubbled in tall fancy glasses topped with slices of fruit.

"Aah, there you guys are."

"Where's Max?" asked Dexter.

"He's headed off to the Ranger headquarters. He's asked me to take you to look at the horses."

Swallowing quickly, Abigail shook her head vigorously and stepped back from the manager.

"No. I want to know what's happening about the Rhino."

"Max will tell you when he gets back. Now come along both of you. Let's head to the stables. It's just a short walk."

Grabbing the girl firmly by her arm, the manager pulled Abigail away from the lodge.

She just had time to place her drink on the nearby counter and give Dexter a quick look over her shoulder.

Seeing Abigail's pale face and wide eyes, Dexter sighed and followed them.

CHAPTER 16

Sitting on her usual spot on Ntombi's rump, Jabu swayed in time with the schloop of her feet. Tubi was between her ears looking hopefully inside one for his favourite Bite-you snacks in the form of a fat Tick, of which Ntombi now had rather a lot. Not that Tubi was complaining, and even Jabu had a few now and then. Ntombi stopped abruptly, causing both Tubi and Jabu to wobble on her back.

Ruffling his feathers Tubi gave a chirp, as he righted himself on top of Ntombi's head and peered over her uninjured oval ear. "Hey! What gives?"

"Look! What's that?"

A hard and black surface crossed the path, looking in both directions they could just see the end disappear into the far distance. Its dark shiny surface glinting in the sun, as it hugged the contours of the earth.

Ntombi put her nose close to the tar road and sniffed. "YUCK! It smells disgusting."

Lolloping over, Jabu too gave it a whiff and then picked at it with a slender finger, certain that something tasty could be found underneath. The strange black rock refused to move. Giving a grunt, Jabu used her sharp teeth and bit it. Spitting the disgusting taste from her mouth, the Baboon glared at it and shook her scruffy head.

"It's nasty. Let's go back."

Slowly, Ntombi placed one foot in front of the other. It felt hard, solid, and warm under her feet, so different from the dusty track that they had followed here. She had only taken a few steps onto the ebony road when a clattering, banging van shot past at a terrible speed, rattling loudly, and blasting strange clanging music, that seemed to make the van bounce in time. It whizzed down the road, its rear end belching a cloud of dark noxious smoke. Rearing up, Ntombi spun around on her back legs and galloped away from the ebony track, as fast as she could go.

They hadn't gone far when another van came roaring up behind the first. It whisked past and then came to a screeching halt. A tall up-right human leapt from the rattling van and the drum heavy thumping—*Doph, Doph*—sound of music rever-berated through its rusty metal canopy. People were crammed in, and their loud screeching voices ricocheted through the small trees to Ntombi's swivelling ears.

Ntombi snorted and swayed on her feet, the whites of her eyes stark against her wrinkled grey face. On top of her back Jabu and Tubi screamed, "Run!"

Not needing any more encouragement, Ntombi spun and raced across the road and into the bush, crashing through the scrub as thorny branches scraped against her thick hide. She skidded to a halt in a shower of dust. They're back to get me, thought Ntombi, her heart pounding and breath coming in short gusty gasps.

From a nearby tree, Tubi twittered to his friend, "It's okay, Ntombi. It's gone."

Gasping from her bumping rodeo ride through the scrubby thorn trees, Jabu clambered down Ntombi's back and sat with a thump in the dust, resting her hands on her knees. "Let's get away from that."

They chose a secluded spot to hide, under the overhang of an immense boulder. Melting into the shadows, Ntombi pressed her back against the soothing warmth of the rock, reminding her of the comfort of her mother as they lay together near the waterhole. She didn't think it possible, but Ntombi longed to see the familiar scowling face of hook-snout, the unmoving granite rock formation of her home territory. Try as she might, Ntombi struggled to rest. Her eyes darted left to right as she peered out of the shadows into the brightly lit dry scrubland in front of her.

On her back, Tubi folded his head under his wing and Jabu's soft snorts mingled with the Flies buzzing around Ntombi's festering ear.

Ntombi rested her square snout on the ground and gave a tiny shaky sigh.

"Mama? Gogo? Where are you?"

The stables were a short drive from the lodge and already the sweet smell of hay mingled with the sweat of the horses. Abigail clutched the side of her seat and only climbed out when the lodge manager opened her door after he had pulled the truck to a stop in front of the paddocks. The stables that housed the horses were a lot rougher than the ones back home, consisting of a few large black poles and a tin roof. One of the horses nickered gently as a woman dressed in the green Ranger's uniform and carrying a weathered saddle walked over. She placed the saddle on top of the paddock poles and turned to greet the visitors.

After the usual African handshake, Vusa the lodge manager turned to Abigail. "Kids, this is Gift. She's a horse Ranger here and is off on patrol."

Taking Abigail by the hand, Gift handed her a piece of carrot.

"This is Kazi."

Hand trembling slightly, Abigail held out her flat hand for the chestnut Gelding, who nuzzled at her fingers as he gently took the carrot from her outstretched hand.

"That's an interesting name. You're a handsome boy, aren't you?"

"His full name is Mzilikazi, after one of the Matabele Kings."

The gelding sniffed at her as Abigail stroked his neck. His coat shone bronze in the afternoon sunlight. For the first time since her mother's accident, Abigail breathed in the horsey scent, the bristles on his muzzle tickling her hand.

"You're a greedy boy, aren't you?"

Whilst Abigail was stroking the gelding, the Ranger busied herself with tacking him up, checking the girth under the saddle and the chin strap of the bridle before leading him away from Abigail, towards the mounting block. With a quick wave, she turned the chestnut and trotted out of the yard bouncing as she went.

Coming up behind Abigail, Dexter placed his hand on her shoulder.

"You okay, Abs?"

"Yeah, but Gift needs to sit up more."

They watched together as the mounted Ranger disappeared in a cloud of dust, only turning when the sound of another vehicle came up behind them. The youngsters shouted when they saw Max climbing out of the green Landy and rushed over to greet him, both talking at once. "Max, what happened?"

"They've lost the Rhino calf, but they managed to catch that poacher. He's being questioned now."

"Oh, that poor baby. All alone without its Mamma," said Abigail.

"How can a Rhino calf just disappear? She's still a baby; but a big baby," said Dexter.

Looking at the faces of his young guests, Max quickly changed the subject. "I see you've met the Horse Rangers. They are an important part of the anti-poaching team here. Horses can go places that a vehicle can't."

Still wringing her hands, her thoughts on the little lost Rhino, Abigail nodded slightly. "Yeah. The tack looked a bit rubbish though."

"Not enough money for fancy stuff here, Abi," replied Max.

Shoving his hands in his pockets, shoulders hunched, Dexter turned to them. "Can we go back to the lodge now? My Nintendo should be fully charged. I hate these smelly creatures."

"Why did you come then, Dex?" said Abigail.

Shrugging, Dexter ambled towards the Land Rover, kicking the dust and grabbed the side of the ladder. "I thought you might need me."

Joining her brother on the back of the truck, Abigail thumped down and looked at him as if he'd just sprouted a large horn out of his head. "What? Why?"

"I dunno. You're different here. Not so stuck up. And I know that being with horses is hard for you."

Still staring at him, a smile playing at the corners of her mouth. "Thanks. Why did you come on the trip though?"

Another shrug from the slight pale boy sitting next to her. "Theo is kind to me, and he's the only father I've ever known."

A familiar figure stood in the large doorway of the main thatched building as they drove up to the lodge. Squealing, Abigail flung herself out of the truck and into her father's arms. "Daddy you're back."

"Hello, you two."

Hanging back a little, Dexter stood, shoulders slumped, kicking up dust with his once white trainers. Pushing his daughter away, Theo turned to the boy and gave a smile. "Hi, Dex. How've you been? Come on, I've got gifts for you both."

Boxes and packaging were scattered over the floor and table of the lodge. The other guests looked up frowning as the excited shrieks got louder and louder. Smiling at the commotion, Max tried to shush his guests. He chuckled when Dexter's shout had a large woman tut loudly.

"A drone. Cool."

Also finding the children's enthusiasm amusing, Theodore helped the boy open the box.

"I thought that with your gaming skills you would like this. You'll get some great video footage."

Still smiling at the boy and his stepfather, Max was interrupted when a waiter approached and whispered into his ear. After nodding to the waiter, he excused himself and walked towards a Ranger standing in the bar.

When he returned two faces turned eagerly in his direction, but one look at his flushed face told them that it was not good news.

"Max? The Rhino?" said Dexter.

Ignoring Dexter, Max looked at Abigail and held out a shaking hand, his jaw clenched. "Give me your phone, Abigail."

"No. Why'd you want my phone?"

Slamming his hand down on the table, Max struggled to control himself. "I said, give me your phone."

"But—"

Jumping up from his seat, Theo came to his daughter's rescue and stepped between the furious guide and the defiant girl. "Back off. You can't speak to her like that."

"Well, your precious daughter posted images of the Rhino and didn't take the geotags off as I asked."

"How the hell do you know that?"

"The captured poacher has confessed that's how they located the Rhino. It's these spoilt brat's fault."

Prying the phone from Abigail's hand, Dexter deftly flicked through the screens, when he found what he was looking for he looked up at Abigail, his face pale. "Oh God, Abs. I helped you post that."

The quiet confirmation seemed to knock the wind out of Max. Shaking and panting he turned to leave, but Theo tugged on his arm pulling him back.

"Listen here. I didn't pay for this treatment. Apologize at once."

"Keep your bloody money. I knew I would regret taking this safari, from the moment I met you at the airport."

Running his free hand through his hair, Max all but spat his last words. "Pack your bags. Now. You're leaving."

Wrenching his arm free, Max stormed out, leaving Theodore Martin staring after him open-mouthed.

Behind him, Abigail let out a thin wail. Covering her mouth with her hand she fled to her room, gulping down wracking sobs. It couldn't be all her fault, could it?

A hush had fallen over the dining area. Theodore and Dexter glanced around them, and the other guests glanced away, some shaking their heads. One large jowly man with a booming voice stood up and called out, "Get outta here. You're not wanted here."

Spinning around Theodore rounded on the man, his face red, fists clenched at his sides. As he made to storm over and give the man a piece of his mind, Dexter grabbed his hand.

"Don't Theo, please. Let's just go."

Theodore looked at Dexter, who was shaking his head as silent tears cascaded down his face unchecked. Giving a sigh, he helped to gather the boxes and equipment that had been scattered across the table, and they walked off towards their rooms.

CHAPTER 17

Hours later, Ntombi and her friends still lay against the comforting warmth of the towering boulders, the shadows created by the rough rocks hiding them from view. Not able to sleep, Ntombi lay quietly staring at a tree with a bright green trunk, its branches touching the rocks gently.

A little nose appeared on the branch and two little beady eyes peered down at her. They sat there staring at each other, neither one of them wanting to move, a Rhino calf and a rock Hyrax.

Jabu lay stretched out over Ntombi's back, looking like a shaggy carpet. She yawned and opened her eyes to see the Hyrax staring down at them.

"Howzit?"

His voice caused the little critter to dart along the rest of the branch, onto the granite boulder and disappear into one of its dark crevices.

With a little huff, Ntombi tried to see where it had disappeared to. "Jabu. You frightened it."

All the commotion woke up Tubi and he just managed to see the grey-brown back of the Hyrax as it disappeared. He flittered up to the lip of the boulder and peered towards their cave, gently trying to coax them out of their hiding place.

"It's okay. We won't hurt you."

Out of the shadows crept three or four furry rock Hyraxes. They shrank back when Jabu joined Tubi on top of the boulder.

"Yebo, fuzzies. Can you help us?"

Cautiously, one little Hyrax inched forward into the sunlight, its button nose twitching, little beady black eyes darting skywards. "What you want? What you want?"

Sitting on her haunches, her favourite pose, hands on her knees, Jabu lifted one thin arm and pointed to the ground where Ntombi sat, her head straining upwards.

"Our friend needs to find her family."

"Ja, have you seen them?" Tubi chirped in.

Glancing skywards again, some of the other Hyraxes grew more confident and moved around them picking at the small scraggly grasses that grew in amongst the cracks in the rocks, their small sharp teeth just visible as they chewed.

The first Hyrax spoke again. "I am Mbila. You must leave here. Not safe."

A snort came from Ntombi below them, who was now pacing and hopping as she still tried to see whom her friends were talking to. At the squeaked warning, Ntombi gave a puffing snort back against the rock again, as a shiver ran up her spine.

"Why?"

Peeping over the lip of the rock, Mbila the Hyrax shuddered. "Ukhozi."

"What?"

"Ukhozi, the Eagle."

At the mention of the Eagle, the other Hyraxes, scampered from the trees and darted back into the shady rock crevices. Only one remained at the top of the green tree, the dominant male, his eyes staring unblinkingly across the vast cloudless sky and the harsh sun.

Ears moving constantly listening, Mbila tried to explain. "Ukhozi is a hunter of the skies and brings death to our kind. We fear him above all others."

At the mention of the black Eagle, Jabu flinched, remembering a story about how this Eagle would swoop unseen from the sky to snatch an unsuspecting Baboon from the ground.

"My mama told me stories of the swooping death. It—"

Suddenly a high-pitched mewing filled the air and Mbila gave a startled squeak and disappeared as a shadow sped down from the skies. A pair of sharp black talons glinted red against the sun, pinning Jabu on the rock, as she struggled to free herself from the powerful black Eagle. Bravely, little Tubi flapped and pecked at the Eagle, trying to get him to release the Baboon. Ruffling his glossy black feathers against Tubi's barrage, as if he was nothing but a Fly, he bent his regal head. Jabu's terrified face reflected in the golden-brown eyes, yellow-black tipped beak open. It was only when Ntombi bellowed, that the Eagle peered down at her from on top of the rock.

"Ukhozi, please let her go," begged Ntombi.

Ruffling his feathers again and loosening his talons slightly from around the scrawny Baboon's neck, he blinked slowly at Ntombi. "You are Ntombi?"

"Yes, sah."

"Aah, Farai told me about you."

Trembling, Ntombi's eyes widened at the mention of Farai the Fish Eagle who had tried to help them a few days before. Under the vast claws, Jabu squirmed and screamed, causing Ukhozi to glance down at his yellowish feet and reluctantly released her. "Oh! Shut up."

Turning, his head swivelled back to the little Rhino who sat trembling in the shade below him, as Jabu scrambled out from underneath him.

When Ukhozi spoke again his tone was soft but serious. "This place is dangerous. You must leave."

"But—"

"No buts. Go back across the black track."

"Those uprights and their death-spitting sticks are there."

"More are here, Ntombi. This is deadly territory. Now go, quickly."

Jabu and Tubi had already turned away from the Eagle and were making good their escape. Turning to follow her friends, Ntombi glanced back at the majestic Verreaux Eagle.

He opened his wings and then closed them again, ruffled his glossy black feathers and sighed. "I cannot leave you alone. Follow me, I know someone who can help. He's not far."

"Why are you helping me?

"Your mother, Lindi, once helped me. Now come."

"But what about Tubi & Jabu?"

Opening his wings again, Ukhozi took to the sky with a few flaps, screeching to Tubi and Jabu to follow him.

The Oxpecker and the Baboon heard the screeches and turned to follow as Ntombi broke into a lumbering trot to follow Ukhozi.

In the distance the recognizable thud of helicopter blades filled the air, spurring the trio of friends on. The sound filled them with dread, and they hoped that their trust in Ukhozi was not leading them into more danger.

When the Eagle finally stopped, perching on top of the skeleton of a tree, Ntombi and her friends were gasping for breath. The Eagle waited for them to catch up. As Ntombi, Tubi and Jabu collapsed in a heap, he opened his wings and took off again.

"Wait here."

As her breathing slowed, Ntombi looked around them. The trees stood silent and bare of rustling leaves. Perched on a single stark tree, the Vultures sat hunched, beady eyes watching the friends.

Shuddering, Ntombi shrunk away giving a little squeak. "I no like this place."

"Aiy, Aiy. What are those ugly flappers waiting for?" said Jabu, pointing at the Vultures.

From between Ntombi's ears, Tubi gulped and inched towards Ntombi's large ear.

"Death. They're waiting for death. Look alive."

Shuffling to her feet in the dust, Ntombi made to look as alive as possible by sniffing at the dried crusted piles of dung that littered the ground. A faint Rhino scent still clung to the sun-bleached lumps of processed grasses. She shuffled from pile to pile, hoping to get a fresh whiff of her lost mother.

Behind her, Jabu flicked through the piles, grunting, and smacking her lips when she found something tasty.

"Aiy! Look at these."

Looking at the bleached white objects, a massive skull at one end, Ntombi noticed there were more remains scattered around. In the middle was the dried and cracked remains of an old water hole.

"What is it?"

A gruff voice from behind had them spinning around as a colossal Rhino, with an impressive horn, strode towards them. "Those were once Lumber beasts."

Gulping, Ntombi and the others stared at the new arrival, the Rhino bones completely forgotten.

Then the familiar voice of Ukhozi sounded from a nearby tree. "Swazi will help you now. Hamba Kahle. Go well."

Backing away from the bull Rhino, Ntombi searched for an escape route, not wanting to anger him. The last big one had chased them. He strolled towards the friends and stopped when he saw the fear in their eyes.

"I won't hurt you," he said gently.

Remembering the manners that her mother taught her, Ntombi went up to Swazi. Her head low, she chirped quietly and gently touched his horn with her nose. "Hi. Do I know you?"

"I am your father, Ntombi. But come, we must hurry."

"Wait—What?"

Ntombi's mouth hung open as she stared at Swazi's angular rump, already walking off, expecting them to follow. Looking at her friends and back at Swazi, and then at the countless bones scattered around the area, a wind swirled amongst them leaving a trail of dust and leaves. Mouth still wide open, Ntombi jumped when Swazi gave a loud snort.

"Buya, you three. Come."

Picking their way carefully through the scattered remains, trying not to disturb them, a hush fell over the three friends, Ntombi dragged her feet through the sand, kicking up puffs of dust.

Eventually, Ntombi took a deep breath and trotted up to Swazi as the question buzzed in her head. "Baba?"

"Yebo, little one."

"What happened to those Lumber beasts?"

"Killed by Uprights and their death-sticks."

"Why didn't they get you?"

"I'm only here looking for you, Ntombi. We must hurry. They are everywhere."

Ntombi crept towards her father, nudging his flank with her nubby little horn, she looked up at Swazi as he towered over her.

"Baba?"

"Yebo."

"I'm hungry. Can I have a suckle?"

"Aiy, little one. No. I don't have what you need."

Giving her a gentle push, Swazi hurried her along, knowing that she needed the safety of the crash and the female Rhinos, who would perhaps help with the suckling.

High above them in the towering castle formations of the granite hills, a human watched them.

Through the sights on his rifle, he saw the length of the male Rhino's horn. It was too far for him to get a shot, but he grinned and reached for his phone and sent a brief text message.

The headsets in the helicopter were silent except for the occasional sniff from Abigail, who sat in the back next to Dexter. Both were staring out of the domed Plexiglas windows.

In front, Theodore sat slumped in the seat next to the pilot, groaning slightly.

Max cast an angry sideways glance towards him as Theodore sat shivering, even though it was still warm out and beads of sweat glistened on his brow. "Theodore, you don't look well."

Shaking his head and clutching his light blue coat closer, Theodore turned a shade of green.

Frowning slightly, Max pointed to a small compartment just below the control panels. "Sick bags are there."

Reaching into the compartment, Theodore pulled out a brown paper bag and placed it over his mouth breathing heavily, shakily covering his mouth as his nausea subsided. "Oh! I feel rough."

"Did you take malaria prophylactics and cover up at the river?"

Shaking his head weakly, Theo gulped down another wave of nausea. "No time."

"A good thing you're leaving early."

In the back of the bell helicopter, both children were subdued and silent, except for the occasional sniff from Abigail. The girl certainly knew how to dramatize things, thought Max, remembering the scene earlier. He felt a small pang of guilt; they were just kids, albeit spoilt ones.

Max opened his mouth to speak into the headset to her when another voice cut in.

"Echo1. Do you copy?"

"Go ahead, Bravo2."

Sitting bolt upright, Dexter strained to grasp the conversation between Max and the disembodied voice. He nudged Abigail in the side with his elbow and pointed to his earpiece and mouthed the word "Rhino" to her.

Dabbing her eyes with a crumpled tissue, Abigail leaned forward in her seat as Max ended the conversation abruptly.

"Stand by Bravo2."

The silence in the cabin was deafening. Dexter and Abigail were desperate to know what was going on but after the scene earlier neither knew how to approach Max, who looked lost in thought.

A minute later Max cast a brief look at Theo who was slumped against the side of the helicopter. He looked pale but otherwise seemed okay.

The Ranger base had just informed him that an off-duty Ranger had spotted a Rhino calf trying to cross the Mapisa-Town road. The Rangers had asked if he could take a look from the air.

"The calf's been spotted, we're gonna do a flyover. Won't take long. Okay?"

Punching the air behind Max, Dexter dug in his bag for his new drone and holding it lightly, he switched it on, knowing that this would be a great filming opportunity. "Yeah. That's awesome."

"Get this right. Once we locate it, I will call it in. Then I'm taking you directly to the airport."

Finally finding her voice, Abigail brightened and blew her nose on the tissue. "Okay. Max?"

"Hmm?"

"I'm sorry. Let's save that Baby."

"We'll keep a lookout for her."

The girl smiled, wiped her eyes, and dug out her phone to film, making sure that she had switched to flight mode. With a satisfied sigh, she turned to scan the terrain below, knowing that her phone's GPS tracking was switched off.

The cockpit was a flurry of activity, as Max pulled on the cyclonic stick to bank the chopper towards the long black tar road.

In the back, Dexter programmed his new drone. It hadn't taken him long to figure out how to operate it; it hummed and whirred, capturing the ground below as it whizzed past.

Hunched over the controls of the helicopter, Max squared his shoulders, they'd been searching for over an hour, and so far there had been no sign of the calf.

"It's getting late. Time to get to the airport."

"No. Just a little longer. Please, Max!" begged Abigail.

A slight groan came from Theodore, and Max glanced at him. For most of the flight the man had slept, occasionally shivering, and muttering about the heat.

"My fault. Not kids."

Touching Theodore lightly on his arm, Max whipped his hand back. The man was scorching.

"Okay, Theo? Do you need help?"

"Hmm. Okay," muttered Theo.

"Are you—"

A shout erupted from Dexter, he was pointing excitedly, tapping the window of the chopper. "What's that? There?"

Squealing, Abigail lurched over Dexter, phone in hand to film below.

The helicopter banked towards the grey shape that was running helter-skelter across the parched earth below.

"It's her," said Abigail.

"Wait. Look, behind her," yelled Dexter, bouncing in his seat.

"It's the bull," gasped Max.

A flickering red-orange glint caught the corner of Dexter's eye and he squinted into the sunlight. Then he saw a distinctive shape.

"What's that? It looks like another helicopter."

"What! There shouldn't be any other aircraft around," gasped Max.

"It's very low."

"Can you see any identification numbers or anything?"

"No, but it looks like it is a bluish colour. No, wait. It's brown or Khaki."

Looking through binoculars, Dexter tried to get a good look at the chopper, but it had disappeared completely. "I've lost it."

On the opposite side, Abigail still had her binoculars, watching the Rhino. The helicopter had banked and was now heading towards the Rhino.

"It's here. I see it. It's much bigger than this chopper."

"Let's check it out," said Max.

Heading in the other chopper's direction, Max flicked an open-air channel on his radio, hoping to get identification or at least communicate with its pilot.

The radio crackled but the unknown aircraft didn't respond, except to bank back in their direction.

As it turned, Max saw why Dexter had been unable to identify its colour. It seemed to be patched with panels from different coloured helicopters, so it was blue, red, khaki, and green.

"I haven't seen one in ages."

"Seen what?" demanded Theodore, groggily.

"That chopper. It's nicknamed k-car. It's an old military chopper used in the liberation struggle."

Suddenly, it banked again, bringing it side-on and they all saw several men sitting in the shadows. Bright flashes of light shot out of the door.

"Max!" shouted Dexter. "They're shooting at us!"

Flicking a switch in front of him, Max called over the radio.

"Bravo2, Bravo2. We are under attack. Over."

Ntombi: A Rhino's Story

CHAPTER 18

Ntombi stood frozen like a rabbit in headlights as the menacing metal bird swerved in their direction, the wind from its rotating blades blowing gusts of dust into their eyes.

Nothing Jabu and Tubi did could move the hefty Rhino baby, only a rough nudge and snort from Swazi was enough to motivate Ntombi. "RUN! Ntombi."

The urgency in her fathers' voice galvanized the little Rhino and she lurched into a rambling gallop, almost unseating her rider, Jabu, as they weaved across the grassless plains, desperate to escape the helicopter and the dangerous humans it carried.

Suddenly, gunfire exploded around them. Ntombi reared up and Jabu tumbled to the ground, in a tangle of legs and arms. She shrieked and screeched, curling into a ball as the Rhino bull careened over her, rolling Jabu between his bulky feet.

The sounds of the helicopter and the pounding of Swazis' heart drowned out Jabu's screams.

Rat-a-tat. Ak, ak, ak.

Flapping furiously to keep up with the crazed Rhino, Tubi chirped gratefully when he noticed they weren't the target. "It's not after us."

Sure enough, bursts of fire spat furiously from the second helicopter, the sinking sun glinting red on its windscreen adding to its menace. The first helicopter weaved and ducked, bullets whizzing past it.

Bouncing to a stop, Ntombi sucked in a breath, but Swazi had other ideas and butted her with the point of his horn.

"NO! Don't stop. GO!"

Ntombi broke back into a run with a yelp and Swazi steered her towards a cluster of granite boulders, hoping that would give them shelter and a little safety. They were both gasping when they finally reached the balancing boulders and wedged themselves amongst their rough warm crevices.

Flopping down, Ntombi looked around suddenly realizing that Jabu was no longer perched on her back.

"Jabu? Where's Jabu?"

She made to scramble up, but the big bull placed his chin gently but firmly on her back, forcing her back to the ground.

"Let me go! Jabu! I must find her!"

"No! It's not safe. I'm sure she's not far behind."

Thumping his muscular square rump down, Swazi acted as a barrier against the outside world.

Sobbing, Ntombi lay shuddering in a little heap when she felt a comforting peck from Tubi. "Tubi? Do you know where Jabu is?"

"She was on your back. I'll look for her. Uprights don't bother me."

Off flew the little bird and Ntombi watched as he flew up through the rocks and disappeared out of sight.

In the red Bell helicopter Abigail and Dexter could just about make out the Rhino figures as they raced towards a granite kopje.

The light was fading fast. It was one of the biggest things that Dexter noticed in Africa. Unlike the setting sun in the Northern hemisphere, which seemed to gradually glide into the earth, in Africa, it was swallowed by the earth, in one quick gulp.

Pulling on the cyclic stick, Max struggled to avoid the barrage of bullets from the other helicopter, then it was gone. Whipping his head from side to side, Max tried to get a glimpse of where the strange aircraft had disappeared to. "Where is it?"

"Max! Watch out!" screamed Dexter.

The patched helicopter reappeared to their left, dangerously close. Bullets pinged off the Bell helicopter. Lurching in the air, Max struggled to gain control, and swore when another bullet hit the side of the helicopter with a thud.

"MAYDAY! MAYDAY! We've been hit."

Not waiting for a response, Max held on tight to the stick as the helicopter's alarm sounded through the cockpit and the dials on the instrument panel went nuts, spinning and spinning.

From behind Max, Abigail started to cry. She gripped Dexter's arm so tight that her nails bit painfully into his flesh.

Shrugging her off, Dexter had to shout to be heard over the squealing alarm. "Max! What's happening?"

"The tank. Its hit. We're losing fuel. Fast."

Struggling with the stick and pumping on the pedals, Max desperately tried to regain control. Beside him, Theodore groaned, barely registering the trouble they were in.

Max scouted the darkening ground below them and spotted a suitable landing pad. Not perfect but it would do. "Brace yourselves. I'm going to have to bring this bird down."

They thumped to the ground with a crash, the rotating blades still spinning.

The landing skids bit into the hard soil and the helicopter flipped upside down, its passengers tossed about like salad in a bowl.

As if in slow motion, Dexter watched as his water bottle and the drone flew past his face. Sky and ground seemed to tumble with them until with a loud jarring crunch, they hit the earth and came to a halt. The helicopter lay in a crumpled heap, the screeching alarm finally silenced. The sun dropped and darkness surrounded the downed chopper.

The Rhinos lay undetected amongst the granite kopje, as the world around them seemed to reverberate with the sound of the battling humans.

When the deafening crash bought an end to the terrifying sounds, Swazi cautiously scented the air, ears twitching. All was quiet.

An acrid smell clung to the air, but it seemed stagnant.

Shivering against her father, Ntombi's heart pounded in her chest. She just knew that the death uprights that got her mother were back for her. There was no sign of Jabu or Tubi, and Ntombi was certain that she would never see her friends again.

With a groan, Swazi heaved himself to his feet. "We go now."

Swazi set a merciless pace, not letting up, pushing Ntombi. When she showed signs of flagging, he'd snort and give her a shove. Constantly rotating his radar ears, they crashed through the bush, listening for the sounds of the death uprights, the humans.

Jostling through the thorny scrub, Ntombi's feet dragged in the grey dust, the weariness seeping into her bones. Fluid leaked from her eyes and her head hung so low that her wide mouth scraped at the dust by her feet.

"Baba. So tired. What about Jabu and Tubi? Stop."

"Do you want those uprights to get you?"

"I no care."

Ignoring Ntombi, Swazi pushed on regardless.

It was pitch black when they reached the long ebony track. Swazi stepped onto the tar road, not giving it a moment's thought. He huffed in frustration when Ntombi froze, placing her feet squarely on the ground and refusing to budge, even when he gave her a little poke with his horn. "What now?"

Ntombi's eyes were so wide that they were rimmed with white, her legs quaking. "N-n-noisy c-c-clatter-bangs."

"There are no clatter-bangs now."

Giving the little Rhino a push, Swazi shoved her towards the road.

Ntombi dug in her heels and squeezed her eyes tight, waiting at any moment for a raucous vehicle to slam into her. The bull's weight and size were no match for the undernourished calf as he propelled her across the road. "NO! NO!"

The track felt rough against the soles of her feet, they could withstand the thorns and brittle grass but were still remarkably sensitive. Suddenly the strange sensation of the dark track ceased, and she felt the familiar puff of soft earth beneath her feet.

"It's over," said Swazi, gently pushing Ntombi. "Come, the boundary's not far."

Ntombi opened her eyes slowly, one at a time, blinking into the night. Nothing had happened. No thumping, jangling sound. No humans at all. She glanced at the mammoth shape of Swazi and a memory popped into her head of Balega, the other Rhino calf from the crash, who had been so eager to meet the great Swazi. What would he have thought of this stern and imposing Rhino that had appeared out of nowhere?

"Come. Not far now."

Plodding along weakly, Ntombi walked in the direction that Swazi indicated, just a little in front of him, kicking dust as she went, head hung low. Swazi sighed, he could see that his young daughter was exhausted and that he had found her not a moment too soon.

To Ntombi, the trek towards the silver fence seemed to take forever. She was finding it harder and harder to lift her feet and Swazi kept having to nudge her. The silver wire glinted in the darkness for as far as the eye could see on both sides of the gaping hole in front of them.

She did not question why there was a hole in the barrier.

Swazi glanced around and pushed her through. "Hurry! Quickly now."

Stumbling, Ntombi's foot caught on the broken strands, and she kicked out in a panic as she remembered the last time she had crossed this strange phenomenon.

"Steady."

Halting suddenly, Swazi snorted, head up, radar ears swivelling, stepping protectively in front of Ntombi. His tall horn pointed skywards menacingly.

"Uprights!"

The bush erupted from behind them.

Rat-a-tat-tat. Ack, Ack Ack.

"RUN!" yelled Swazi.

Pushing his daughter roughly in front of him, Swazi snorted, urging her into a gallop. They spun off to the side, weaving through the sliver-leafed Terminalia trees, Swazi puffing along behind Ntombi as they fled once again, feet hammering the dry earth.

Suddenly, Swazi grunted. He screamed in pain and slammed to the ground, his wide mouth dragging in the dirt before he shuddered to a stop.

Turning on her heel, Ntombi ran back to him. "Don't stop, Ntombi. Run!"

The terror in his voice had Ntombi jerking back into her loping gallop, swerving to avoid the tree that had just exploded from bullets biting into it. She heard a yell from an upright and the deathstick clattered to the ground and fell silent.

The sounds of the humans and their guns faded into the night the further she got from them. Fear and adrenaline urged Ntombi onwards. She slowed her pace but kept going, aimlessly drifting through the bush. Alone for the first time, she gave a mournful squeak. Maybe Jabu and Tubi were nearby and would hear her calling.

"Jabu? Tubi? Jabuuuuu? Tubiiiiiii?"

Ntombi: A Rhino's Story

CHAPTER 19

Breaking into a run, Dexter caught up with Abigail as she weaved through the Terminalia trees and scrubby Acacia. "Wait, Abs. We need to check the direction."

The girl came to a stop, and Dexter stared at the Southern Cross constellation, mentally visualizing the imaginary lines from the bottom of the Cross to the pointer stars to find south. "This way."

Taking the lead, Dexter marched off, constantly checking they were going the right way.

A little surprised at Dexter's sudden authoritative command, Abigail broke into a jog following his torchlight as he led the way through the bush.

Over the past few weeks, both Dexter and Abigail had come to realize that the African bush was seldom quiet at night, and tonight was no exception. With no buildings or glass to deaden them, the sounds seemed to be amplified as their footsteps crunched on the dried leaves: chirping Crickets, hooting Owls, trilling Nightjars, and the squeak of Bats as they whizzed through the air. The distant roar of a Lion made Abigail jump and she inched closer to Dexter.

"Is that a Lion calling?" she said, casting a furtive glance behind her.

"I guess so. Don't think it's close. Check for a phone signal," said Dexter.

"Yeah. Good idea, Dex."

Holding down the power-up button, Abigail's face illuminated with a hazy blue light as it flickered on. She gave a frustrated groan when she saw that there was still no signal. Holding the phone, she climbed on top of a small cluster of granite rocks, hoping that a little height would be enough.

"Anything, Abs?"

A sudden snort had Abigail freeze, "What's that? Give me the torch, Dex."

She flicked the torch from side to side, lighting up the area. She squeaked when two shiny blue eyes blinked at her out of the darkness.

"What is it, Abigail? Lion? Hyena?"

"Quick! Use that banger thing."

"No. Wait, Abigail. It's—it's a Horse!"

"What?"

Clambering down from her rocky perch, Abigail slowly approached the animal, whispering to the wild-eyed creature, who whickered in return.

"I think it's that Ranger's horse. Wasn't his name Kazi?"

"Where's its rider then?"

Patting the sweaty flank of the chestnut Horse with one hand, Abigail reached up with her free hand and grabbed the reigns.

Meanwhile, Dexter flicked the torch through the bush, trying to find the Ranger.

"Hello. Anyone there? What was the Ranger's name, Abs? Present or something weird like that."

"Gift. Wasn't her name, Gift?"

"GIFT!" called Dexter.

There was no response, just the distant whoop of a Hyena.

"Let's go, Dexter. The rider could have fallen off miles from here."

"Yeah. Let's go. That Hyena is getting closer."

Tugging at the reigns, Abigail made to lead the horse away, when Dexter grabbed at her sleeve.

"Wait. Surely it will be faster if we ride Kazi?"

"I don't think I can. It's been too long."

"We can do it. Max & Theo are counting on us. Surely this will be so much quicker. Besides, Kazi will know the way back to the Lodge."

"Oh, God. I hate it when you're right."

Once Abigail had calmed the knocking of her knees, she placed her foot in the stirrup and bounced onto Kazi's back. Reaching down, she helped Dexter clamber up behind her, and kicked the horse into an easy canter.

Face pressed tightly against Abigail's back, Dexter clung on as he flounced about, thinking perhaps this wasn't such a good idea after all. "Slow down, Abigail! SLOW DOWN!"

"Sorry, Dex. Forgot you don't ride. Do you—"

"Stop. What's that? Can you hear it?" whispered Dexter, fumbling in his top pocket for the scarer.

A faint squeak came from a thicket of acacia trees. Abigail took the torch from Dexter, bunching the horses' reins in her other hand. Kazi didn't seem to be concerned and immediately dropped his head to chomp on a small patch of grass.

"Kazi's okay with it. I'm sure horses can sense predators," said Abigail.

Casting the light around, Abigail gasped when she saw the tiny Rhino calf standing in the centre of the beam.

Ntombi blinked at them, hardly moving, almost as if she no longer cared what happened to her. Her breath came in short gasps as she tried to get the scent of the creature that stood silently in front of her.

"A Stripy-beast. But where are its stripes?"

Edging the horse forward, Abigail felt Dexter shift to peer around out from behind her.

Taking a tentative step towards the stripe-less Zebra, nose scenting the air, Ntombi snorted softly. What was this creature? It certainly smelt a bit like Dube the Zebra, but there was another scent.

The Rhino took another step toward Kazi, Abigail, and Dexter. As she stepped more into the light, they got a better look at her. Ntombi's thick grey skin hung from her frame, and deep folds of skin collected around her legs. Every single rib jutted out and Flies hovered around a wound that was once her ear, a putrid smell seemed to linger in the children's nostrils.

"Oh no," gasped Abigail.

The whispered sound of Abigail's voice was enough for Ntombi, and she jerked her head up when she realised that the strange scent belonged to the upright-humans. She spun around and lumbered out of the light and out of sight, her footsteps fading away.

"What do we do, Dex? This is all my fault. I must help her," said Abigail.

"Follow her. She's going south."

They cantered slowly after Ntombi, Dexter bumping around on the horse's rump, clutching at Abigail's grubby shirt, whilst trying to keep track of the stars that were guiding them south.

"Stop! Let's check directions," called Dexter.

Abigail was just pulling up to a stop, when the horse suddenly snorted in fear and threw his head up. A Hyena gambolled out of the shadows towards them. Kazi reared up and spun on his hind legs.

Dexter, still clinging to Abigail, slid off the horse's rump, taking Abigail with him. She landed on the ground with a thump, cracking her head on a nearby tree. Then the world went silent.

Ntombi could hear the stripe-less Zebra's hoofbeats behind her and she tried to quicken her pace, but her feet felt heavy and the burst of adrenaline that had fuelled her—urging her on— fizzled out like a flame on a matchstick. She fumbled through the bush with her head held high, inhaling the scents with every shallow breath. Whipping her head around, she caught a whiff of odour. Not uprights with their death stick. She breathed in again. Not human. A whooping sound reverberated in her torn and injured ear. The Hyena. With a snort, Ntombi forced her leaden feet into a rambling trot.

Suddenly, the earth beneath her gave way and she felt herself falling. The warthog burrows beneath her had collapsed, and the termite mound that had once stood proudly above the warthogs' lair crashed in on top of the little Rhino, knocking the breath out of her.

"Oomph."

Gazing upwards, Ntombi struggled a little to free herself. Pictures of her mother, followed by Tubi and Jabu, and finally the father she hardly knew, filled her head. Mama, I'm alone now, she thought. With a squeak and huff, she laid her head on her legs and waited for the Hyena to claim the rest of her.

"Go away, Dexter" said Abi, groggily, pushing at the face breathing in her ear. "Your breath reeks."

"It's not me."

With a jolt, Abi's eyes opened, and she stared into the glinting dark eyes of a Hyena as it sniffed around her, its rancid breath making her gag. Screaming, she scrambled to her feet, causing the Hyena to leap back in shock, clearly not used to having its potential food suddenly come to life so noisily. Waving her arms, she ran at the creature.

This was too much for the cowardly animal. It turned and fled, tail between his legs, cackling as he went.

"I'm not dead," yelled Abi, throwing a rock after it, then she turned on Dexter. "Why didn't you use the bear thing?"

"Can't find it. Must have fallen out of my pocket."

Breathing heavily, she realised that her head was thumping. Shakily she reached up and rubbed her head, wincing when she felt a lump on the back of her head the size of a golf ball. Her head felt warm and wet. She pulled her hand back in shock and could just make out the smear of fresh blood on her hand. She swayed dizzily on her feet and placed a hand on the nearest tree to steady herself. Pulling her shoulders back and sticking out her chin determinedly, she put one foot forward and then the next, walking unsteadily away from the tree, stumbling over a small termite mound.

"You okay, Abs?" asked Dexter, he stood dusting himself off.

"I'm fine. We must get going. Can you see the horse?"

"No. Poor thing was terrified. Wait—Look, here's the bear banger!"

Looking up at the sky, Abigail noticed that the stars were fading away. Where had the Southern Cross gone? Panicking, she did a 360. Without the Cross, how were they going to find their way?

"Sun's coming up. What do we do now without the Southern Cross?"

Bending onto a knee in the dirt, Dexter looked at the rising sun and drew a rough compass in the sand.

"Sun rises in the east and sets in the west. North, east, south, west. This way."

Staggering after Dexter as he broke into a jog, Abigail weaved her way through the trees. Time was running out. They had to get help.

She hadn't gone far when she walked around a towering termite mound—almost as tall as she was—and there lay the Rhino calf. It lay, barely breathing, totally exhausted and didn't even react when she slowly reached out to stroke it gently on its back.

"Oh, you poor thing. Just look at the state of you."

Looking up past the Rhino calf, Abigail called out to Dexter, who screeched to a halt and joined her on the other side of the little Rhino, touching it gingerly. Its skin felt rough but warm, its breathing shallow, not flinching at their touch.

Ntombi opened her eyes to look at the upright walkers who crouched at her side at the base of the collapsed warthog burrow. With a faint huff and a wisp of dust, Ntombi closed her sunken eyes, allowing sleep to take her again.

A crack from above had Dexter scrabbling out of the dented ground, the blue metal tube—the scarer—already in his hands and loaded. They had come so close to a Hyena attack; he wasn't going to make that mistake again.

As he stood above Abigail and Ntombi, he heard the unmistakable click of a rifle being loaded, and without a second thought, Dexter released the catch as the projectile shot up into the air.

Bang!

Another bang echoed through the bush, and Dexter hit the ground covering his head with his arms.

"Stay down, Abigail," he screamed.

Abigail had already flung herself over Ntombi, and then a voice shouted.

"Stop. You are surrounded."

"Wait. We need help."

Standing up slowly, Dexter raised his hands above his head as a man in olive-green fatigues stepped towards him, rifle aimed at his chest.

"Please. We are tourists from the Dwala safari lodge. Our helicopter was shot down. Help! Please!"

CHAPTER 20

Ntombi's eyes blinked open. As her senses awakened, she shook her head, trying to clear her blurry vision. Lights and shadows seemed to dance in front of her eyes. An overwhelming stench filled her nostrils—Uprights. Frantically, she scrambled to her feet, her mind urging her to run. With her body rocking and rolling like a ship on a rough sea, her floundering legs constantly trying to catch up, she scrambled to get away from the smell of humans. Then her legs gave up completely, and Ntombi tumbled to the ground, dust wafting around her.

331

Watching the Rhino calf struggling to get up, Abigail rushed forward to help, but Max, leaning heavily on crutches, stopped her.

"No, Abigail. Leave her. The anesthetic is wearing off."

"But she needs help."

"The matriarch won't like you getting too close. It's not her baby but she will still try to protect her."

Snorting, Ntombi tried again to get her disobedient legs to work. She had to run. They were back. She had just managed to totter to her feet again and she stood breathing heavily, eyes wide. Then she heard a familiar squeak.

"Ntombi. It's all right girly."

"Gogo?"

The head of the Rhino crash, Gogo the matriarch, sauntered over to the young calf and nuzzled her gently.

"You are safe, little one."

Nearby, the girl gasped and clasped her hand over her mouth, whilst her stepbrother, Dexter, used the hand controller to position the drone over the Rhinos, filming their gentle greeting.

Blinking her eyes yet again, Ntombi felt sure that she must be seeing things, but there stood Gogo, more rotund than ever. The old female Rhino's flat horn was now rounder and taller than Ntombi remembered, but otherwise it was her. Resting anxiously on her haunches, Ntombi's legs still slightly unsteady, she squeaked back in delight. "But how—? Swazi?"

"Is okay. Kangela. Look."

Behind Gogo, the ginormous bull Rhino Swazi, was busily chomping swishy grassy snacks as if there was no tomorrow.

Scampering around him was Balega, Ntombi's older cousin, bombarding him with questions and being a general pest. "Where've you been? How'd your horn get so big? Are you staying?"

"Balega. Leave Swazi alone. Come greet Ntombi," said Gogo, sternly.

The young bull Rhino, Balega, looked briefly in Ntombi's direction with a brief nod, "Howzit, Ntombi." Then he turned back to worship his hero, Swazi.

Looking up from his grazing, Swazi ignored the younger bull and limped towards Ntombi.

The bull walked stiffly and Ntombi could see a jiggered scar across his shoulder. "Yebo, Ntombi. You scared us."

"You were hurt?" said Ntombi.

"I'll live. Your ear? It is better?"

Rotating her radar-ears, she listened for the sounds of the bush; the Cape Turtle Dove, the chomp of the other Rhinos as they grazed nearby, the churr and tsk of a yellow-billed Oxpecker. "It's shorter. But it works."

The rest of the Rhino crash, Ntombi's family, came over to greet the young Rhino in turn, squeaking and touching her nose.

"NTOMBI!"

A nearby familiar chirp and tsk had Ntombi looking around, her head swivelling from side to side as she looked for her feathered friend.

Then there he was, popping out of Balega's ear, smacking his red and yellow beak together.

The little dusky brown bird flew over to land on Ntombi's head between her ears.

"His Bite-yous are not as nice as yours."

"Tubi! It is so good to see you."

Looking around again, Ntombi wondered where the scruffy Baboon was, with her bright amber eyes, and kinky tail? Ntombi was certain she would be nearby scratching through the piles of pongy dung, searching for her favourite crunchy snack of Dung Beetles.

"But Tubi. Where's Jabu?"

"Maiwe. Ntombi, I'm telling you it was too terrible."

"Tell me. What?"

"Well, I went back to look for him, after Swazi hid you from those very bad uprights. It took me a long time to find him."

Shaking his brown head sadly, Tubi continued. "It was too late. He is no longer with us."

"Aah. Poor, poor Jabu. It is my fault. I dropped him."

Thumping down onto her bottom, Ntombi's shaking legs no longer seemed able to carry her.

In frustration, Gogo snorted at the Oxpecker, showering Tubi with Rhino snot. "Enough. I told you not to upset Ntombi. She needs to eat and rest. Now hamba—go."

Gogo pushed Ntombi towards a shady spot under a dark green tree, where Sisi, Balega's mother, had just settled her ample body comfortably. "Come Ntombi. Sisi will give you a little to drink. Balega will share."

Still a bit woozy, Ntombi did as Gogo told her and lay down next to Sisi, closing her eyes. The sweet smell of milk woke Ntombi from her fitful sleep.

"Mama?"

The smell overwhelmed Ntombi and she nuzzled at the warm body that lay next to her, slurping hungrily.

"It's okay, Ntombi. You have a good drink."

Breaking off suddenly, a droplet of milk clung to her lips. That voice wasn't her mother's and Ntombi glanced up into the kind face of Sisi.

"But—Mama? I want my Mama."

"Your mother would understand. Now drink more."

The milk was delicious and creamy and Ntombi smacked her lips as milk oozed from her wide lips.

Looking up from where he sat with Swazi, Balega noticed the attention that Ntombi was getting from his mother.

He rushed over and pushed Ntombi away. "Get away. She's my Mama, not yours."

"Balega. You can share. There's plenty. Besides, you're older and can eat a swishy snack. Now leave Ntombi alone," said his mother, Sisi, sternly.

With a huff, Balega flopped down next to his mother, glaring at Ntombi, but he allowed her to snuggle down next to him and his mother.

Ntombi closed her eyes against the midday sun and fell asleep.

From their spot not far away, the humans watched with interest.

Tears sprung into Abigail's eyes, as she clasped Dexter's sleeve.

"Look. She's suckling. Is that her mother, Max?" Abigail asked.

"No. It's the other calf's mother. I've never seen this before. Truly amazing. But she'll need a lot more. She's very undernourished."

"Undernourished? She's only been separated from her mother about a week," said Dexter.

"Ja. However, like human babies those first few weeks after birth is important for a Rhino calf's development, not to mention the all-important bond that is established between mother and baby. Hopefully, when we re-introduce the mother back into the crash, that bond won't have been lost."

"Oh, I hope so too," said Abigail, her eyes still on the now sleeping Rhino calf.

"Why do you only hope, Max? Surely you know the outcome?"

"This is a new technique and has never been done before. Dr Ben Moyo and his team of vets are pioneers. Over the next few days, all we can do is watch and hope. Come, let's leave the Rhino to snooze, Theodore will be back from the hospital soon."

Two days later, Ntombi was snoozing fitfully under the dark-green leafed Gardenia tree, the first few buds of its creamy white flowers filling the air with their sweet scent. A large truck rambled through the Safari Park and came to a halt.

The crash snorted and huddled together as uprights scuttled about like ants. A strange hefty metal box was rolled off its back, it rocked on its rollers, as something from inside snorted.

Snorting and swaying from side-to-side, Ntombi looked for Gogo and ran to her side as soon as she spotted her. Pushing Ntombi behind her, Gogo told her, "Stay here, little one. You'll be safe."

From under Gogo's rotund belly, Ntombi watched as the strange rock thing opened and out staggered something that resembled a lumber beast. It looked like a lumber beast, it smelt kind of like a lumber beast, but a different smell mingled with her own scent. Where the horn should have been, was a large divot of sunken skin and crumbled bone.

"Who's dat, Gogo?" said Ntombi, lifting her nose to its scent.

"Maiwe! It can't be. It is Lindi!"

"Mama," whispered Ntombi, as she caught the familiar musky smell. "MAMA!"

In a state of shock, mother and daughter stared at each other for a frozen moment. Then Lindi stepped forward to gently touch her calf on the top of her head.

"Where your horn, Mama?"

"Gone, little one. My, you have grown. But you are too skinny."

"Your horn it come back?"

"No. Not this time."

The screams of the girl echoed through the hills. From the lodge, the guests watched in horror as a fellow guest was escorted by the local police.

"No!" screamed Abi. "Tell them, Daddy. Tell them it's not true."

Reaching for the hysterical girl, Theodore looked pleadingly at the uniformed man next to him. "Let me say goodbye. I will come peacefully."

He turned to give Abigail and Dexter a last hug. "Be good. The police have said that if I co-operate, I'll get a reduced sentence. I'm sorry, kids. I'm so sorry."

"Why? Just tell us why?" asked Dexter.

"I had a deal go wrong and one of the shareholders offered me a way out."

Taking charge, Max hobbled on his crutches over to the youngsters as Theo was bundled into the waiting police van. "You don't need to see this. Come. Let's go to the office where we can talk."

Once the children were seated, and Abi's shuddering sobs reduced to the occasional whimper, Max explained to them what had happened. How someone had approached their father and offered him money to take his family on safari and get the locations of the Rhino. Max had become suspicious when Theo only showed an interest in Rhinos with horns. Theodore himself had confirmed it when he was delirious with malaria. "I had no choice but to report it. Your father is right. If he can provide more details on the poaching ring, he should be out in 2 years."

Running a shaking hand through his hair, Dexter looked at Max, his face white. "What will happen to us?"

"I have recommended that you go to boarding school at Mapisa."

"What about my mother? Won't she come and get me?" asked Dexter, as he wiped his wet face on the bottom of his T-shirt.

"We will have to wait to hear more from your fathers' lawyers."

Leaning forward in his seat, Max pinched the bridge of his nose and took a steady breath before he continued.

"Look. This is not going to be easy for you but try to understand; Theo made a mistake and now he must pay for it. Even grown-ups make mistakes, but the trick is to own up and take responsibility."

"I never want to see him again," sniffed Abi. "What he has done is unforgivable."

From the platform above the watering hole—the same spot where Max had taken Abigail and

Dexter only a short time ago—they watched with bated breath as the large truck delivered its precious cargo to the Dwala Safari Park. Once the Rhino had safely wandered off with the rest of the crash, it closed its huge steel box and drove away.

The female Rhino was severely scarred, and she still had a long battle ahead of her. The gaping hole in her face where the horn used to be would have to be kept under constant surveillance to avoid infections. The vet team wanted to try a technique where they graft elephant skin over the top of the hole in Lindi's face.

Letting out his breath, Dexter flicked the switch of the drone's controller, bringing it back around toward them to land gracefully in front of them. "That's one tough Rhino. To think what she has been through."

"I know, Dr Ben did an amazing job, completely revolutionary."

On the other side of the Rhino crash, a herd of Zebra grazed alongside the anti-poaching horses, Kazi content amongst his striped cousins.

On seeing Kazi, Abigail remembered the first time she had seen the chestnut gelding. "Max,

Ntombi: A Rhino's Story

what happened to Gift, the Game Ranger that rode that chestnut?"

"We still haven't found her. We suspect that she may be caught up with the poachers."

"Oh no. That's terrible."

"Ja. She may have no choice if she or her family have been threatened. We'll continue to look for her. The poachers can be ruthless."

"Yeah. We've seen that first-hand."

"Max, did they manage to catch the ones that shot you down?"

"Well," started Max.

After they had shot down the helicopter, the poachers headed for the hole in the fence, they had spent the day watching the Rhino and knew exactly where to find them. The poachers hadn't anticipated that the Rangers had increased their vigilance and were surprised to come under fire. As a result, several poachers had been shot and the others had been captured and were awaiting their trial.

"But what of the other chopper?"

"Sadly, there's no sign of it. According to the poachers who were questioned, it belongs to a government vet. He has been paid big money to bring in Rhino horns and was able to purchase that old air force helicopter. This enabled him to get to the more remote parks easily. However, he did have some help with locating them."

"It helped him get away, too," said Abigail.

"Possibly. Unfortunately, not all vets are as dedicated as Ben Moyo."

Just then, the vet himself walked up the steps to join them. He was trailed by another man in a suit, looking very out of place in the bush, sweat beading down his forehead.

"I must hand it to you brats. You came through in the end. This would not have been possible if it wasn't for the exposure you got us on social media. We have been inundated with offers of extra funding."

"Will the mother Rhino be okay? Won't she need her horn?" asked Abigail.

"We're hopeful that she will be okay. But it's early days, we will have to monitor her closely. Mother Rhinos do use their horn to protect their young but that is where the funding comes in. We can pay for extra Rangers to protect them.

345

Besides, Lindi—that's what we've decided to call the mother—will be able to nourish her little girl Ntombi, and then go on to hopefully have other young. Very important when a species is on the brink of extinction."

"Ahem." The suited man cleared his throat.

As if noticing the man for the first time, Max offered his hand to the other man. "Aah, Mr. Sibanda. Thank you for coming. Kids, this is your father's solicitor. Do you have news?"

Both Dexter and Abigail swung around to the man, suddenly serious, as they waited for the man to tell them the fate of their father and themselves.

"Yebo. I have news. Your father has been given a reduced sentence of 2 years, due to his assistance with capturing one of the middlemen."

Gulping, Abi nodded. "What about us?"

"Your aunt will fly over to meet you, but it looks likely that you will both be sent to Kestrel boarding school in Mapisa."

"What about me?" said Dexter. "Is my mother coming?"

"We have not been able to locate her. You will go also and then come here in the holidays."

"Is that true?" asked Abi. "We can come back in the holidays?"

"Yes. But you will be required to work here in the trust," replied Max. "It will be hard graft. Are you up for it?"

Abigail and Dexter looked at each other and then back at Max.

"You mean—" started Abi.

Max nodded.

"Yeah!" shouted Dexter, punching the air.

"I take that as a yes then," smiled Max, knowing it was only the beginning.

TRACY LEE MAY

Born and raised in Zimbabwe, when her nose wasn't buried in a book, Tracy spent her childhood wandering through the bush in search of nature, either on foot with her falconer father or on the back of a horse.

As a grown-up, Tracy spent a few years after secretarial college, working in boring office jobs until her and her partner, now husband, decided that the bush was where they should be.

Together, they trained as Safari guides and blissfully spent the following years showing guests their version of Africa and sticking fingers in elephant or rhino dung.

She now lives in the UK with her family and springer spaniel.

ACKNOWLEDGEMENTS

I am grateful to all who have helped and supported me during the very lengthy process of writing Ntombi.

I am thankful to my children Amber and Courtney and my husband Brian for their endless love and support.

And finally, to my mentor Julie who has helped guide and mold me into a better writer.

Dear Readers,

In 2015 I watched in horror with the rest of the world the story of Hope, a White Rhino who was a victim of poaching. The Saving the Survivor charity worked endlessly to save Hope. We all watched as this brave rhino fought against all odds and clung to life even though she had lived through a traumatic experience.

It was Hope's story and my own experiences working with Rhino when I was a safari guide in Zimbabwe that sparked the idea for this Ntombi.

If you would like to know more about what Saving the Survivors do or help in any way their details are on the next page.

Best wishes

Tracy

Saving The Survivors

A registered charity in South Africa, Namibia, The UK and the USA. Saving the Survivors was founded by Dr. Johan Marais in 2012 to treat and care for Rhino who had fallen victim to poaching or traumatic incidents. This included Rhino that have been wounded, as well as victims of snaring and other trauma. Whilst we are best known for our emergency work with Rhino, we also treat any other endangered species in need.

The Saving the Survivors team regularly works with Lion, Leopard, African Wild Dog, Sable and Roan antelope and Elephant, to name but a few. In addition to this, we manage and deliver many proactive initiatives such as community and breeding programs, human-wildlife conflict mitigation and wildlife translocation. Most of these animals are being treated in the bush in their natural environment, as transporting them is not always possible, and it is often extremely stressful.

We work throughout Southern Africa, but we also aid endangered species worldwide. If you would like to donate to the project, please click the donate button or visit –

https://www.savingthesurvivors.org/

Here you will find all methods of donating including Card payments, PayPal and bank transfers.

Tracy Lee May